Making Peace and Nurturing Life:

An African Woman's Journey of Struggle and Hope

By

Julia Aker Duany

"God grant me the serenity to accept the things I cannot change, the courage to change the things I can, and the wisdom to know the difference."

ISBN: 1-4107-6281-5 (e-book)
ISBN: 1-4107-6282-3 (Paperback)

Library of Congress Control Number: 2003094021

This book is printed on acid free paper.

Printed in the United States of America
Bloomington, IN

1stBooks - rev. 06/25/03

Photo on page 257 "Syracuse v Wisconsin" by Steve Parker (1999).

Maps on page 257 adapted from United States Central Intelligence Agency map of Sudan (1994), courtesy of Geography-Map Library at Indiana University, Bloomington.

Author Cover Photo: Talbot Studio, 318 N Union St. Bloomington, IN 47401

This memoir, *Making Peace and Nurturing Life: An African Woman's Journey of Struggle and Hope*, is written in loving memory of and dedicated to my father Benjamin Bil Lual Machar, my mother Roda Atiel Machot, and all the southern Sudanese people who lost their lives in the struggle of our homeland. It is also dedicated to many southern Sudanese people who are searching for peace. It is further dedicated to my family, sisters, brothers, nephews, nieces, and my many, many relatives.

CONTENTS

Our Home: The Sudan

This is our Home,
Let peace dwell here,
Let the land be full of contentment,
Let love abide here.

Love of one another,
Love of humanity,
Love of life itself,
And love of God.

Let us remember
That as many hands build a house,
So many minds make a nation.
This is our Home, The Sudan.

Julia Aker Duany

Julia Aker Duany

FOREWORD

As each of us lives our lives, our greatest opportunities arise from the people we meet and with whom we learn to work. As a teacher and a scholar, it has been my great privilege to have met and worked with many others who have come to Bloomington, Indiana, to participate in what we call a Workshop in Political Theory and Policy Analysis. Colleagues in the United States Agency for International Development recommended Michael Wal Duany to come to the Workshop as a visiting scholar to pursue a course of study that might contribute to opportunities for development in his homeland. Wal, his wife Julia, and their children came to Bloomington in 1984 and became residents of the university community. This began the process of long and fruitful discussions about the meaning of life among the Nuer and the Nilotic peoples of southern Sudan.

We as human beings are in many ways strange and extraordinary creatures. What distinguishes us from all other creatures is the way that we have created languages and how each of us becomes whatever we are able to achieve through our use of language. We acquire language from those who nurture us as soon as life begins. Ways of life are embodied in what people have learned and transmit to others from one generation to another. The vernacular that is learned from those who care for children is gradually extended through further experiences of learning and using languages that endure as long as life persists. Toward the end of the twentieth century, for example, life is being transformed by inventing, learning, and using new versions of languages that might be referred to as computer languages or machine languages.

Once we acquire skills in the use of words that stand for general principles and abstract ideas, it is easy to spin out fantasies of the imagination that lose touch with reality. When that happens, life becomes a struggle to discipline our imaginations by the way that ideas get related to deeds.

A great problem among human beings is to try to appreciate languages. The proper uses of a language shape ideas and deeds in tragedies and successes that people are able to achieve. Our challenge is how to develop mutual understandings that can serve as a basis for being helpful to one another. In the course of time, Wal Duany completed a doctoral dissertation about the way of life lived by the Nuer people in southern Sudan. By deepening his own understanding of his own people and their language community, he has better prepared himself to cope with struggles that have engaged his people and the other peoples of Sudan. This is his way of contributing to developments in Africa.

While working with Julia Duany, who shared many of Wal's concerns for her people's interests and the more general interests of humanity, it occurred to me that a memoir as a reflection on her own life's experiences would be a way for others to gain a deeper understanding of what it would mean to be an African woman caught up in the turbulence of the world in the latter half of the twentieth century. Julia was born of a Dinka mother and a Nuer father. Both the Dinka and the Nuer are identified as among the Nilotic peoples of Africa, which means that those people have had some association with the Nile River and the Rift Valley that traverse the length of the eastern African continent. The open Savannah that extends across the African continent beyond the Sahara Desert is also known as the Sudan. The Republic of Sudan is at the intersection of the Nile River and the grasslands of the African Savannah. The term *Sudan* in its original Arabic meaning refers ambiguously to the "country of the blacks."

Julia's memoir enables each of us to use our sense of empathy and our imagination to put ourselves in her place and to begin to appreciate what it would mean to live along the Nile River as it traverses the grasslands of sub-Saharan Africa and to begin to appreciate what it would mean to be an African woman. As we come to an appreciation of such a way of life, we acquire some sense of a shared community of understanding through which we can learn to be helpful to one another.

Some of us may presume that the United States government, other governments, and international organizations of governments can act as our proxies in addressing the problems confronting other peoples of the world. There is a grain of truth in such a presupposition but that grain of truth is apt to be mixed with a greater degree of fantasy than reality. Government to government relationships may be a way of fashioning a system of cryptoimperialism that is less than helpful in enabling peoples to cope with the basic exigencies of making peace and nurturing life.

Apart from their place in a university community, the Duanys gained an understanding of American life by the way that they and their children came to share the experiences of other children and parents in acquiring the learning, experience, and skills associated with schooling. That experience did much to give them an understanding of the American way of life and to enable parents and children of others to gain an understanding of some of the skills and capabilities of Nilotic peoples. The Duanys through their association with the Presbyterian Church gained access to another facet of people to people relationships that transcend national boundaries. These are opportunities available to each of us to draw on our appreciation of what Julia Duany has to say in *Making Peace and Nurturing Life* to extend our horizons of understanding by relating to others who come from different lands and cultures; share our schools, churches, and places of work; and relate to us and our children. These are the circumstances where we make peace and nurture life. In my life as an American of Scandinavian descent, I have become persuaded that each of us is who we are by using our facilities with languages to learn from others. We learn how to reciprocate by being helpful and contributing to the learning of others. By such patterns of reciprocity, we each take our place in making peace and nurturing life as an alternative to seeking opportunities in which people war on one another.

Reading memoirs, autobiographies, and biographies is an essential complement to other forms of discourse. What Julia has to say immeasurably deepens my understanding of what it would mean to be an African and of the importance of working with African colleagues who will take their place in shaping the future of African civilization. I recommend the adventure to you as a way of coming to appreciate the opportunities that are open to each of us.

Vincent Ostrom
Indiana University, Bloomington

PREFACE

My name is Aker Bil Lual, and my Christian name is Julia. My family name is Cieng Jak of Lou Nuer, which was handed down from my father's great-grandfather. Although my father was able to read and write, he did not think it was important to remember all the birthdays of his thirty-two children. My mother told me that I was born in a town called Rumbek during the mid 1950s. I grew up in a small village called Akot, thirty miles east of Rumbek. Akot, being close to Rumbek, had a semblance of town life. I grew up around relatives and traditional elders, speaking only the Dinka language. Later I went to a boarding school run by Catholic nuns in a big town called Wau and, like many other Nilotic people of my generation, tried hard to learn the modern ways of life. Eventually I went on to college, taught at the primary and secondary levels, and traveled around the world.

In the Africa that was my world, elders who knew and practiced our ancestral ways of living lived. Even then there was a sense that Africa was changing so fast that it was in danger of losing its traditions. They still live, but their ways are fading. My mother fears that too many young people like myself are assuming the Western ways. And why shouldn't we? The nuns at school punished us if we spoke our native language. They discouraged all signs of the Nilotic culture and way of life. We were even told by the nuns, especially during traditional events, not to associate ourselves with "the villagers," as they called them. We often felt ashamed to be with our people and to practice our culture.

It was not until I attended college that I began trying to understand the life of the Nilotic people. Although I spent most of my time as a young woman studying in northern Sudan, I never lost the foundation of Nilotic tradition that my parents had taught me. I now am a mother of three sons and two daughters. I gave my older daughter an ancestral name, Nyagon (Gon woman). Gon is the largest section of Lou Nuer. This is a name she inherited at birth from a great-grandmother. Graduate school encouraged me to find pride and meaning in my ancestry. Now I try to practice my culture and raise my children as Nilotic people.

From following the ways of my people I have come to value the teachings, stories, and daily examples of living which they have shared with me. I pity the young Nilotic girls and boys who, as they struggle to survive in the rapidly changing world of Africa, will miss knowing the older elders of the Nilotic people. Because I remember how much their knowledge helped me when I was younger, I am putting together this book to serve as a message from a Nilotic mother to her children. This is my tribute to the Nilotic people and their culture.

I am writing in an effort to fill a space in history that has been left empty for too long. Although many books have been written about the Nilotic people, only a few of them were written by the Nilotic people themselves. Most books tell about Nilotic warriors, cattle raiding, and wars. Some overlook the importance of women in the societies. Readers of these books might assume that the Nilotic women lived boring lives of drudgery and had limited experience. In reality, their lives were rich with stories. This is a book written by a woman telling the story as it is.

I am also writing this book because I want to understand myself and my place in the world. I want my people to recall the faces of their loved ones and friends who were killed in civil war. We are survivors, and it is our responsibility to speak out so that the genocide, abuse, and torture will never happen again in this world. We must tell our children and our children's children. The future generation of southern Sudan must learn about the stories and the survivors— the heroes—and then do their part to help make the world a better place. This means teaching peace, repentance, forgiveness, and reconciliation, not retaliation.

I hope this book provides some inspiration and guidance to the young people who are growing up after me in the Nilotic world. I also hope that it enlightens many other readers by showing that Nilotic women have the knowledge to make a contribution to world history. I think it would help the present African situation if we all learned to value and respect our own ways of life, as well those of other people.

I know my world. I know who I am—a mother, a future grandmother, a real Nilotic, and above all a Nuer woman—a woman of this modern world.

ACKNOWLEDGMENTS

The one who throws the stone forgets; the one who is hit remembers forever.
Angolan proverb

To hope is to see peace in the face of anger. Peace is not the end; it is always to be continued. The one who forgives gains the victory.
Yoruban proverbs

With love I thank my parents for the challenge they gave me when I was growing up. My mother has always provided me with a strong example of kindness and generosity combined with hard work and devotion to her family. For my mother, family care is humanity. She taught me the skill of good parenting, which, as a mother of five, I have found to be the most rewarding experience of my life. My mother raised five children of her own (two sons and three daughters) and five nieces and seven nephews. She also was a leader to all of my mothers (my father's other wives). Her home was a center for many relatives. When I was small we all lived together in a number of cluster-huts built by my father and my maternal uncles. My father died in 1982 at the age of 69 and my mother died in 2002 at the age of seventy-five.

I never dreamed of writing a memoir, because I thought I had nothing to write about. Then one day Professor Vincent Ostrom, who had been writing on human relations and democratic societies, encouraged me to write my life story. As result of his encouragement, I am proud to present you with my story.

I am deeply grateful both to my people and the other Nilotic peoples (whose influence remains strong) for helping me to understand the process of making peace. My understanding of peace is not an absence of war, but rather a way of life. Courage, dignity, brotherhood/sisterhood, ambition, responsibility—these are needed today as never before in Sudan and in Africa as a whole. We must cultivate them as tools for completing the task of establishing human equality, freedom, dignity and common decency.

I wish to express my deep sense of appreciation for the Workshop in Political Theory and Policy Analysis at Indiana University and especially to Professors Vincent and Elinor Ostrom, who, as co-directors, took a deep interest in my desires and made it possible for me to write this memoir. I shall never forget their loyal and devoted services as my academic advisors.

I am grateful to the Rockefeller Foundation for their financial sponsorship of my dissertation field research in 1993. I am also grateful to the Center for Mission Research at Maryknoll for their sponsoring my contribution to a 2000-2002 study of grassroots Christian communities' response to violent conflict. Both of these experiences enabled me to gain deeper understanding of the cultural, political, and social issues, and to develop ideas for practical solutions to problems in Sudan.

I appreciate the editorial assistance given by Professor Gilbert Weldy, Dorothy Weldy, Sarah Colburn, David Willson, Tom Hargis-Young, Margaret Polski, Brenda Mathews, and Isabel Hogue. I am grateful to Professors Patrick O'Meara, Frances Stage and Robert Arnove for reading and comments. I also appreciate receiving help from Patty Dalecki, Gayle Higgins, Linda Smith, Paula Jerrells, and Anne Leinenbach and sharing ideas with African visiting scholars Dr. Bamidele Ayo and Dr. Cheibane Coulibaly. I owe a debt of gratitude to Dave Adams for offering his wisdom, encouragement and support, not only to me, but also to the cause of peace in southern Sudan. Finally, I offer special thanks to my family—my husband Wal, our five children Duany, Nyagon, Kueth, Nok and Bil, my niece Thongdiar and nephew Ger, who have demonstrated patience and understanding when Mom was so often preoccupied.

I hope this book will be a magic that leads my people to peace—"a magic that occurs when one human being helps another." Sometimes at night, I shut my eyes tightly, hoping that somehow, when I open them again, I will see my people living in peace.

I just want them to be free.

With Love,

Julia Aker Duany

INTRODUCTION

The glory days of armed struggle against oppression are over. In Africa, untold millions of people have lost their lives and nothing has been achieved, particularly in the Sudan. It is clear that violence as a political strategy has failed to improve people's lives.

Images of My Homeland

Africa is the second largest continent in the world. It is home to more than one tenth of the world's people and, anthropologists believe, is the very cradle of human civilization. Africa's people supply the world with cocoa, coffee, tea, palm, cotton, rubber, sisal, and more. Africa's land is rich with minerals, diamonds, gold, natural gas, and petroleum. Yet, after more than 500 years of contact with the Western world, in the minds of many people in the West, Africa remains the Dark Continent.

Today, while Western science and technology imagines itself poised on the brink of a glorious millennium of progress, the Western media portray Africa as a land of political, social, and economic instability. It is a land covered by thick jungle and dry desert, inhabited by wild animals and primitive people, and ruled by warlords who kill and enslave their own people. Indeed, in some Western minds, Africa does not exist except as a form of perverse television entertainment called "the news of the day."

Media images portray Africa as a land bleeding with poverty, hunger, disease, malnutrition, and disaster. This Africa has nothing to offer, but everything to receive. This Africa is hopeless. It is a land in need of salvation through international welfare programs. After watching so many images of ethnic cleansing in Rwanda, clan warfare in Somalia, and starvation in Sudan, Western viewers see Africa as a land where coup d'etat is a national sport and there are more AK-47s on the streets than automobiles.

Hand-in-hand with news images are Hollywood images of ignorant, superstitious African natives. My children have seen the old *Tarzan* movies on television, images that make a laughingstock of African culture. These and other stereotypes of the pagan African still compel Islamic and Christian missionaries to convert Africans to organized religion and to Arabic and Western culture. These images are not accurate, because they stand alone, without historical, cultural, political, or any other context.

Media and Hollywood images of Africans exclude the vast scope of human activity. They communicate nothing of the rhythm of life that characterize the herdsmen, the farmers, the women, the schoolboys and schoolgirls, the merchants, and the government officials. They communicate nothing of the ordinary African people who seek a more peaceful and prosperous future. Nor do these images answer the disturbing questions they raise.

The African State

How did Africa, a continent with natural wealth and human potential, become poor, destitute, and unstable? Why do many of Africa's people go hungry in a land of plenty? The answers to these questions are not simple, but they provide some context for understanding the African people—the people of my world—and the modern African State. The seeds of the present social, economic, and political predicaments in Africa were sown, to a large extent, during its colonial period. The resulting crop is depleting the soil base upon which civilization depends, yet people labor on, living off of the harvest of subsidies and the fruit of corruption.

Before the influx of the Europeans, much of sub-Saharan Africa was composed of locally self-governing societies. The Europeans came first as explorers and later became interested in governing Africa. During 1884 and 1895, Britain, France, Belgium, and Portugal divided Africa among themselves without regard for existing racial, linguistic, ethnic, and religious groupings. Colonial frontiers were, and still are, at odds with Africa's ethnic loyalties. The imposed political boundaries divided families and communities and disrupted Africa's social institutions. The colonial strategy of divide-and-rule broke down the African communal spirit.

Colonialism also changed the African economy, as people were expected to produce cash crops or to sell cattle to pay taxes to the colonial government. Most African countries eventually came to produce a single cash crop for export. Ghana now grows about fifty-five percent of the world cocoa supply. Kenya produces tea and Uganda, coffee. Tanzania exports sisal and cashews. Sudan supplies cotton and gum arabic, an ingredient found in ink, soft drinks, and candies.

The colonial period formally came to an end during the 1960s when many African nations won independence. Yet involvement in African economic and political affairs by industrial societies, the Soviet bloc, and some the Asian nations did not end. Africa's new colonial master is the modern multinational corporation, still directing African political and economic affairs.

From ancient times, Africa has been a religious and ethnic melting pot. For example, ethnic inter-marriages still provide linkages and alliances for social cohesion. African religion recognizes God as the source of all life, especially human life. African cultures are built on a philosophy that demands individual participation so that everyone can achieve.

According to African cultural tradition, achievement is vertical. One does well in order to benefit the entire community. Consumption is horizontal, or shared. One works hard to help others. The value of sharing applies to both the individual and the group.

African cultures see that the whole cosmos is a religious and spiritual arena, with spirits interacting with humans for either good or evil. Africa's religious heritage plays a major role in everything Africans do. African theologian John Mbiti has quite rightly described African people as incurably religious. Of the three major religions in Africa—traditional African religion, Islam, and Christianity—traditional African religion is not easily distinguished from cultural, social, and daily life. Traditional African religion reflects a strong belief that nature and the cosmos are a spiritual phenomenon and a living reality. The African's dependence upon and respect for nature gives credence to the full range of life's activities and philosophies. African cultures hold that anything taken from nature must be paid back ten times. People are taught to revere nature and not to expect to receive anything good from nature if nature is badly treated. This ethic reflects learning to live with nature rather than learning to conquer nature.

Many centuries ago, the spread of Islam gave rise to a Muslim identity in Africa. Particularly in the Sudan, Islam became a class religion marked not only by doctrinal positions and religious activities but also by a range of institutions including families, mosques, schools, health and cultural centers, and government itself.

Ancient Christianity and Judaism also penetrated the African world, often blending with indigenous beliefs to form distinct religious communities such as the *Falasha* (Jews) of Ethiopia who claim their descent back to King David. During the colonial period, Christian missionary zeal led to the opening of Africa to the Western world. Christian missionaries built churches, schools, hospitals, and participated in other development programs throughout Africa.

The work of Christian missionaries with vernacular language played an important role in African education. An estimated 800 to 1,000 different and distinct languages are spoken in Africa, including Arabic, English, French, and Portuguese. Having translations of the Bible available in African languages led African converts to internalize the tenets of the Christian Gospel, to expect their God-given human rights to be affirmed by their colonial rulers, and, ultimately, to demand political independence.

After nearly half a century of existence, however, the modern African State has yet to capitalize on Africa's strengths. More than ever before, Africa is shaped by media images that give no hint that those strengths even exist. But they are there. The African continent still has large areas of arable land. The African State still has the potential to change. The African philosophy still says, "I am because we are, and because we are, I am." And the African people are still full of hope and ready to pick up the challenge of recovering their lost identity and wealth.

The Sudan

My home in Africa is in the Republic of Sudan. Extraordinarily diverse, Sudan is the largest country in Africa, encompassing one million square miles of land and twenty-seven million people. Sudan's farthest boundaries straddle Africa's two cultural regions: the Islamic North and the African South. Within Sudan's borders are Africa's vast geographic regions: rain forest, savanna, steppe, and desert. More than 400 different languages and dialects are spoken among Sudan's 597 ethnic groups. Within each of the two major religious groupings—Islam and Christianity— the Sudanese people practice a variety of traditional indigenous African religions.

The history and culture of ancient northern Sudan are distinct yet interwoven with the history and culture of ancient Egypt. Modern Sudan reflects other important cultural influences. Early in the Christian era, some of the ancient Sudanese kingdoms converted to the Christian faith. This early Christian influence was overshadowed after Mohammed's death in 632 AD, when his successors led Arab Muslims on great waves of conquest reaching far into Europe, Asia, and Africa. Politically, the Muslim Empire did not last very long. Nevertheless, an Islamic empire and culture commands millions in Sudan today through the dominance of Arabic language and Islamic doctrine and law.

Though Egypt and Sudan had strong ancient bonds, during the eleven centuries following the rise of Islam many Arab groups came as traders into the land that is now Sudan. There they intermarried with the Africans, creating the present Sudanese society in the North. They became Sudanese, yet most of them rejected Egyptian identity and control.

By 1800, Egypt had determined to conquer Sudan and eventually succeeded. In 1881 a northern Sudanese Muslim proclaimed himself to be the Mahdi, the divinely appointed guide who would drive the Egyptians out. Great Britain and Egypt joined forces to halt the Mahdi's rebellion. This began a period in Sudan's history known as the Anglo-Egyptian Condominium (1899-1955). The Anglo-Egyptian Condominium was an uneasy alliance, dominated by the British. Its purpose was to control the Nile waters.

The Condominium was ruled according to British colonial policy and was administered separately in the northern and southern regions of Sudan. The decision to separate the regions administratively cemented the cultural, religious, and ethnic differences. It also accelerated the economic differences, since the British and Egyptians made the North the focal point of all development and educational ventures.

During the 1940s, a nationalist movement began to arise in the North. Sudan's two powerful northern political parties grew out of that movement. As Sudan traveled the road to independence, African Southerners increasingly felt disenfranchised, betrayed, and dominated by the British-Egyptian

Muslim North. Both northern parties played into the power struggle between Egyptian and British interests. One of the two parties, the *Umma* or Nation Party, represented the Mahdi sect and demanded independence from Egypt. The other party, the *Khatimyya* or National Unionist Party, called for a union between Egypt and Sudan and had the backing of al-Mirghani, head of a powerful Muslim sect.

Eventually it became clear that the Arab North had no intention of sharing power with the African South. Civil war broke out in 1955 and continued after the Republic of Sudan became an independent nation-state in January 1956. Sudan's succession of northern governments could never bring the South under control.

Fighting continued until 1972, when the southern *Anya-Anya* forces signed a peace agreement with the Nimeiry government. Unfortunately this peace, known as Addis Ababa Accord, was doomed from the start because the foundation necessary for a pluralistic, democratic society was not there. Northern policies of forcing the South to adopt the Arab culture and language and the religion of Islam intensified as Nimeiry strengthened Sudan's ties to Egypt and Saudi Arabia.

Throughout the 1970s, the failure of grandiose economic development schemes eventually oriented Sudan away from its ties with the Soviet Union and closer to the Western nations. But even that shift did not abate the ominous tide of internal unrest over consequences of bad economic policies. When reserves of strategic minerals and petroleum were discovered in the South, Nimeiry's government thought it had found the solution to Sudan's troubles. But before he could exploit these new sources of wealth, Nimeiry had to get the country back under control.

Unfortunately for Nimeiry, it was too late in the game for the discovery of oil to change the outcome. By the early 1980s, strikes, riots, and shortages of goods and services had paralyzed the nation. To rally support from the northern parties, President Nimeiry declared an Islamic Revolution. He announced on September 8, 1983 that Sudan's civil laws had been revised to bring them into conformity with *Shari'a,* Islamic Law. Sudan became an Islamic State overnight, putting into force a harsh, eye-for-an eye system of law. In time, the new legal system created a new class of disabled citizens by deliberate mutilation, in particular through the cross-mutilation of amputating a hand and foot. The majority of people who became victims of the Shari'a were non-Muslims.

The declaration of Nimeiry's so-called September Laws also accompanied serious violations of the 1972 peace agreement with the *Anya-Anya* forces, also known as the Southern Sudan Liberation Movement (SSLM). As far as the South was concerned, the government in Khartoum clearly intended to exploit the South's natural resources, particularly the oil, at any cost. Civil war broke out at once. The southern forces, backed this time by the Soviet Union's surrogate in Ethiopia, reorganized in 1983 as the Sudan Peoples' Liberation Army (SPLA). When *Shari'a* was imposed upon the South, the second civil war took on a religious importance that had not characterized the previous struggle.

In 1986, a coup d'etat forced Nimeiry out of power. The coalition government of northern political parties that replaced him was, in turn, overthrown in 1989 by General Omar al-Bashir and Hasan al-Turabi, the charismatic fundamentalist leader of the National Islamic Front (NIF). The NIF outlawed all other political parties and began transforming Sudan into an Islamic dictatorship. In response, the northern parties in exile formed the National Democratic Alliance (NDA), which included the Sudan Peoples' Liberation Army. The common ground seems to be the desire to oust the NIF.

Islam in Sudan

Most of the Sudanese Muslims are of the Sunni sect. The union of religion and identity has shaped the course of Sudan's institutions, international relations, and internal problems. The Sudanese Muslim is bound by his Arab identity more tightly than are other Muslim peoples of sub-Saharan Africa. To be Muslim is to be Arab.

The most serious consequence of the 1983 declaration of *Shari'a* is that it transformed the civil war into a *jihad,* throwing the full weight of northern religious passion and identity behind the struggle to keep the people and resources of the South under control.

In Sudan, Islam carries a significant tradition with regard to *jihad,* or the defense of Islam. On the basis of this tradition, northern Muslims have been incited to invade, kill, burn, and destroy communities for sake of Islam. To the majority of northern Sudanese, there is no distinction between religious and civil law. The *Qur'an* embodies the Law. To the majority of southern Sudanese, however, the *Qur'an* contains some very oppressive rules which today are looked upon as forms of cruelty. Examples of this are the amputation of a thief's hand and stoning of an adulteress.

During Nimeiry's Islamic Revolution, opposition to *Shari'a* was viewed as a threat to the homeland. The extreme to which Nimeiry was willing to go in order to defend his regime is illustrated by the case of Mahmud Muhammad Taha. In 1945, Taha founded a Muslim reform movement known as the Republican Brothers. When Nimeiry began to implement *Shari'a*, Taha his followers opposed it on legal grounds because many provisions violated human rights. Taha was declared an apostate and publicly hanged in January 1985. The Republican Brothers were banned from the country.

Islam in Sudan is used as a vehicle to express ideological, socio-economic, and political cleavages. It has given birth to and nursed many different and competing Muslim identities, such as modernist/traditionalist, urban/rural, and autocratic/populist, as well as to various forms of millenialism. All of these identities, as competing religious and political forces with local and sometimes international connections, are trying in one way another to take over the apparatus of the State in order to serve their own objectives and interests.

The Nilotic Peoples

All African peoples have a strong sense of group identity, a sense of belonging to a great family and of occupying a traditional and historic area or region. The Nilotic people of sub-Saharan Africa received their name because they are the original settlers along the River Nile.

The Nile region includes the area known as the food basket of Africa. It is endowed with vast stretches of undeveloped natural resources, wildlife, and vegetation ranging from savanna to tropical forest. In the region, there are two seasons: the dry season, from November to April, and the rainy season, from May to October. Most agricultural activities take place during the rainy season. The people grow maize, pumpkin, peanuts, sorghum, beans, peas, yams, cassava, and more, as well as a variety fruits and vegetables.

The Nilotic people are found in Kenya, Tanzania, Uganda, and Sudan. They are subdivided into many localized, yet extensive communities. The Nilotic groups are the Dinka, Nuer, Shilluk, Anuak, Bari, Acholi, Lopit, and Lotiko. Their lives center on their cattle. The Bantu groups are the Azande, Kreh, Moru, and Ndogo. These groups are originally from West Africa. They are mostly farmers and herd small numbers of sheep and goats. They are also known as great hunters. The present-day Nilotic and Bantu peoples of southern Sudan still derive their character and way of life from the enduring traditions of their ancestors.

My own people are the Nuer, the people of my father. The Nuer occupy hundreds of miles along the River Nile in northeastern southern Sudan. Its natural waterways provide a channel of unifying communication among the peoples who navigate them. The *Sudd* region—the flood plain of the White Nile—is also their principal source of water. The Nile's seasonal inundation, which supplies life-giving fertility to the area, encourages all who live there to stay there. Cattle are central to lives of the Nuer people. The Nuer move with their livestock on a regular cycle, going to the higher pastures during the wet season and to the pools, lakes, lagoons, marshes, and river channels during the dry season.

The Nuer are often identified as a classic case of an acephalous society—a society without a head. This social structure is similar to that of federal societies, if the term "federal" is construed as pertaining to a covanental society. The Nuer have a strong covanental tradition, but without the formal political apparatus that is commonly associated with the levels of government in a federal system. Customary law among the Nuer holds to traditional ideas of covenant, breach of covenant, and re-establishing the bonds of covenantal relationships.

The Dinka people, the people of my mother, are primarily located in the Bahr el Ghazal region of western southern Sudan. Some Dinka communities of various sizes live in the Upper Nile region and others live in the Kordofan region of western northern Sudan. Like the Nuer, the Dinka are cattle keepers and generally are an acephalous society. Within some Dinka segments, however, more centralizing instruments of government may be found. Certain Dinka clans adhere to hereditary ritual powers and serve as priests whose symbol of office is *Bany Bith,* the sacred fishing spear. Among the priests, a single "master of the fishing spear" is acknowledged as pre-eminent. Even so, the authority of the spear master is slight and both priests and warriors may freely change their allegiance from one spear master to another.

The Shilluk peoples live along the Nile, north and south of Fashoda land in the Upper Nile region of southern Sudan. The Shilluk cultivate the land and keep only a few cattle, sheep, and goats. The Shilluk are a kingdom. Their country is divided into districts, each with its own head, all of which recognize the *reth,* or divine king of the Shilluk.

The Anuak peoples live east of the Nuer at the foot of the Ethiopian escarpment. The Anuak, like the Shilluk and many Lou groups, maintain a *nyiye,* or divine king.

Civil War (1983-present)

The lives of all of Sudan's Nilotic peoples have been touched in some way by the civil war and affected by the Sudan Peoples' Liberation Army. In 1991, the SPLA split into factions, largely along ethnic lines. The South was virtually destroyed by the in fighting that followed the split. Peoples who had lived side-by-side for centuries suddenly turned modern weapons upon each other, burning villages, raping women, kidnapping children, and stealing cattle. The fighting caused an enormous refugee problem, displacing many thousands of Nilotic peoples from their homelands and livelihoods.

There were many reasons why the SPLA broke up. One was over ideology. The best known rival to SPLA to emerge from the split is the South Sudan Independence Army (SSIA), led by Dr. Reik Machar and later known as the United Democratic Salvation Front (UDSF). Machar's group advocated the South's right to self-determination, in contrast to John Garang's insistence upon a united, secular socialist Sudan.

By 1996, the grassroots people in the South had grown weary of the fighting among the liberation movement factions. That same year, Dr. Reik Machar's UDSF and several other southern liberation movement factions signed a peace charter with the

Government of Sudan. That charter was never approved by John Garang and the SPLA. In April 1997, the Government of Sudan agreed to allow a referendum on self-determination for the South. The referendum was to give the South the option of either revising its political relationship with the North or becoming a separate nation. This agreement, however, served only to marginalize Machar and the groups associated with him. It was never implemented by the North.

Efforts to resolve the North/South conflict appear to have reached a stalemate. Peace talks between the SPLA and the Government of Sudan are held sporadically, but continually stumble over the idea of self-determination for the South and the relationship between state and religion. Both the SPLA and the Government of Sudan have held to a strategy of excluding other groups (both northern and southern) from participating in the talks.

The Southern Liberation Movement Turns Tyrannical

The greatest challenge to unity among Southerners is posed by John Garang, the leader of the SPLA. He has committed himself to "total social revolution." This means that anything belonging to the past is "anathema and must be destroyed." The SPLA attempts to psychologically reconstruct individual members of society. It attacks traditional Nilotic values and the authority of parents and elders through the use of terror. The process of reconstructing society through terror involves a coercive stripping away of the traditional bases, structures, and values that shape and guide an individual's life until he or she becomes an isolated unit. Then the individual is re-educated to accept a series of new precepts, structures, and values. The process undermines a society, causing it to shatter into pieces so that it can be re-constructed along utopian lines.

The SPLA's system of Marxist-Leninist precepts is a social poison. Variations on this theme can be found in Aristotle's analyses of tyranny, the French Revolution, the Soviet Union, Nazi Germany, Mao's China, Pol Pot's Khmer Rouge, and countless modern totalitarian states. In every instance, the elite who led the people into revolution failed to deliver on their promises.

The Sudan People's Liberation Movement advances what I call a garbage agenda. It is a mixed ideological bag proclaiming a united Sudan and a secular state with equal rights guaranteed to all citizens. In 1983, the SPLM/A launched its vision of the "New Sudan," reminiscent of the "New China," but with its own distinctive brand of brutality. After cleansing certain rural areas of southern Sudan, the SPLM and its glorious army commenced to purify the population by eliminating the useless elements.

The SPLM/A reign of terror led to corruption and massive destruction of both peoples and property. Worse, by definition the cycle of revolution could never end. The doctrine of social revolution provides no institutional means of conflict resolution other than coercion, foreclosing the possibility of ever rationally ending the terror. Nor can the system ever change. Opinions that are not politically correct cannot be expressed for fear of punishment, torture, or death.

The structure of the SPLM/A hinges on one man, the Commander-in Chief John Garang. His decisions are made in an arbitrary way, overriding the system of legitimate succession of leaders. And since no leader dares freely express his views, personnel policies are determined on the ground of private connections, intrigue, and manipulation. By forbidding differences of opinion, the SPLA hastens its own demise and downfall.

I cannot recount the thousands of nightmarish stories that I was told by those who have either visited or lived in the SPLA controlled areas. But similar themes emerge in story after story. People tell of being robbed, imprisoned, and persecuted by the SPLA authorities. They tell of being arrested and imprisoned for protesting the insolence of the SPLA comrades.

I have my own horror stories of the SPLA gunmen. In early 1985, my 17 year-old stepbrother and 19 year-old brother were killed in the war. Another of my brothers, Edward Ater, was at one time a commander in the SPLA. He was placed in and SPLA detention camp when he protested the torturing of civilians. Edward and some other men managed to escape. They traveled at night to avoid recapture. While on the way to the Kenyan border, Edward's group ran into and SPLA patrol. The men on either side of him were killed during the shooting. Edward was wounded, but managed to get away.

After four decades of warfare, life has changed in southern Sudan for the worse. People are dying from to what amounts to government-sponsored genocide. The liberation movement has created a harsh environment where the margin between survival and death has narrowed considerably. There are precious few healthcare services available in southern Sudan. A whole generation has grown up without schooling. Land mines prevent the people from using the grazing land, fields, and roads. Theft and disease reduce the cattle population, making families destitute. I have seen so much sadness in the faces of my people. If we wait another four decades for peace, there will no communities in southern Sudan, no Nilotic people, and no Bantu people left to rebuild the society.

Hope for Peace

After the 1991 SPLA split set off a brutal inter-ethnic war among the liberation movement factions, ordinary village women in Upper Nile organized in an attempt to stop the fighting. They set in motion a peace initiative resulting in a number of agreements, including the 1999 Wunlit Dinka-Nuer Reconciliation. I participated in many of these events, experiencing first hand how grassroots women inside Sudan offer primary potential as an agency for change.

Nearly twenty years of war in southern Sudan have permanently altered the social fabric. Now two-thirds of the southern population are female. This demographic shift presents two civic and social challenges. First, women as a group face obstacles to participation in civic life. These include poor health, low self-esteem, illiteracy, cultural bias, and a time-consuming physical workload simply to survive. Second, grassroots women with leadership potential are limited in their effectiveness because they lack training and experience. Their potential will remain untapped unless there is a broad-based effort to equip them with the civic and vocational skills they need to help rebuild society. Unfortunately, the insecurity in the South makes it very difficult for anyone to connect grassroots women with resources, support, and expertise.

In general, peace, relief, and training initiatives in East Africa are coordinated by individuals and organizations on the outside and apart from the grassroots people in the conflict zones. As a result, the initiatives do not develop the talent of local, grassroots people and fail to deliver tangible, long-term benefits. As this trend continues, the capacity for broad-based, collective grassroots community action diminishes, both in initiating and in taking ownership of reconciliation, peace-building, and development. This capacity cannot be imposed upon society from above; it must be built from the grassroots up. In the long-term, institutionalizing the gap between the grassroots and the elite does not bode well for the future of democracy and development in Africa, especially in southern Sudan.

I have spent many years conducting research in the field, interviewing southern Sudanese, and searching for ways to find peace. My findings concur with other research findings from studies of populations worldwide. The overarching concern of grassroots women in southern Sudanese communities is for peace-oriented activity such as food production, road building, education, disease prevention, and health care. The majority of research findings also recognize that women are still playing a central role in the family and serving as "bridge builders" between ethnic communities through inter-marriage. In order to build upon these findings, those women with leadership potential, whether schooled or unschooled, need to be identified and trained so that they can strengthen the role that women play in building peace, civic life, and community development.

In spite of the obstacles, the emerging potential for grassroots peace processes present a real opportunity for the southern Sudanese to apply inventiveness and ingenuity in making peace and in solving their economic, social, and political problems. I am convinced that the primary resources for dealing with Sudanese problems lie within the historical, cultural, and religious context of the people themselves. Thus, the people must build the future by drawing upon the resources of historical village life. To face the ongoing challenge of making peace and nurturing life in southern Sudan, my people need to understand themselves, their history, and each other.

One of the best things that ever happened to me is writing this book. In telling my own life story, I discovered that the Nilotic people are indeed agents of their own lives, that peace is a group effort, and that in the hearts of the Sudanese people there is still hope for the future.

The following lament came from the heart of a mother who shared her story with me during one of my visits to my homeland.

I grew up in the thirty-seven-year-old war in Sudan,
I got married in the same war,
I raised my children in the same war,
I am about to become a grandmother in the same war.

Life will go on, but if the ways of my people perish, then someday someone will read this book and say, "This people had a wonderful culture. Someone should have helped them stop the war, because without land and cattle there can be no Nilotic people."

My promise to my people is that as long as I am alive, I shall continue to speak on their behalf.

The great powers of the world have done wonders in giving the world an industrial and military look, but the great gift still has to come from Africa—giving the world a human face.

Stephen Biko, 1971

My father
Benjamin Bil Lual Machar

Chapter I

Every Life Has Its Story

The building blocks of human societies are families and communities. They nurture in each generation the skills essential to human intercourse in the larger society.

The Ways of My People

I forge an understanding of myself and the world around me. I was born into a large family: father, five wives, and thirty-two children. I also belong, as most Africans do, to a wider extended family, and to the community as a whole. The community among the Nilotic people—Nuer or Dinka—is viewed as the embodiment of reality, a reality present in everything in life. All Nilotic people realize their nature through relationships with others in the community. When I was four years old, I started to follow my mother as she collected firewood, fetched water, milked cows, pounded flour, and took care of my younger brothers and sisters.

My father was Nuer and my mother Dinka. I viewed myself as Nuer, but we spoke Dinka in and outside the home. All I did with my parents was what they knew. I can vividly recall evenings of storytelling around the fire in the village or in the cattle camps. It was mostly the grown-ups telling stories to the children, but everyone was interested and involved. We, the children, would re-tell the stories the following day to other children in the fields while we picked beans or groundnuts (peanuts), followed our mothers clearing the weeds, looked after the calves at the cattle camp, or enjoyed nature along the River Nile.

The great nature provided life, and the stories that shaped our lives. These stories, mostly with animals as the main characters, are full of stirring events, such as the river saving its people from the hot sun of sub-Saharan Africa. Foxes, hares, tortoises, or mice, though small and weak, were our heroes because they were full of innovative and clever ideas. We identified with them as they struggled against predatory brutes like lions, leopards, hyenas, and crocodiles. Their victories were our victories and through them we learned that the apparently weak can find ways to live in peace with the strong. We followed the animals in their struggles against hostilities of nature such as drought, rain, sun, and wind, where a confrontation often forced them to search for means of cooperation. But we were also interested in their struggles the animals often had among themselves. These struggles, against nature, predatory animals, and each other, reflected the struggles we experienced in real life.

The grown-ups did not neglect to tell stories with human beings as the main characters. There were two types of characters in human-centered narratives. One type was the true human being with qualities of courage, kindness, mercy, and social concern for others. The other types were fantasy characters. These characters were often frightening and cruel. There were human-eating humans and two-mouthed, mean types embodying hated and evil doings. They represented qualities of greed, selfishness, malaise, conflict, and self-interest that always worked for the downfall of humanity. These two types of characters

2

personified what was good or bad for the larger community.

Cooperation as the ultimate good in a community was a constant theme. It could unite human beings with animals, like dogs, which were the human's best friend against evil and predatory beasts. Cooperation is illustrated in the folk tale of how a tortoise, who was small and artistic, designed the beautiful colors of zebras, leopards, and other animals who were very kind and treated him nicely. Then little tortoise was threatened by a hyena, which was selfish and demanded for himself the most beautiful colors of all animals. The hyena was mean and cruel to the tortoise. The tortoise, though he was afraid, gave the hyena the ugliest colors of all. The message was clear: threats and intimidation are not the right way to get what you want.

In most of the folk tales, the hero is often a hard worker who uses his cattle (wealth) to support his kin, the poor, and the studious. The hero for a young girl is the mother figure, who is affectionate and toiling constantly for her family. When misfortune strikes, she cries out with tears and with protest, but her love and efforts never flag.

There were good and bad storytellers. A good one could tell the same story over and over again and it would always be fresh to us children. A good storyteller could repeat a story told by someone else and make it more alive and dramatic. The real differences were in the use of words and images, in the inflection of voices, the affecting of different tones, and the way the story related to real human experiences.

Thus, I learned to value words for their meaning and nuance. Language was not a mere string of words. It had a suggestive power well beyond the immediate and lexical meaning. My appreciation of the suggestive, magical power of language was reinforced by the games I played with words through riddles, proverbs, transpositions of syllables, or nonsensical but musically arranged words. I understood that language had a beauty of its own, and also that it was the carrier of my culture, a culture of dignity and human complexity. Language, through images and symbols, gave me a view of my world. At the time, our home, the field, the cattle camps, and the River Nile were my pre-primary learning institutions, but to me, what is important here is that the language of my evening lessons, the language of my immediate and wider community, and the language of our work in the fields and the cattle camps was one.

The social structure I grew up in is that of an extended family. Individuals in the Nilotic society find themselves governed by fixed family relationships that are determined by custom. All relationships are defined first by bloodline, then by the distinction between senior and junior status. The elders have the knowledge and the right to take the lead. The young must listen, learn, and obey.

The relationship between the father and the child is the most important of all the kinship relationships, for it is through the father that the blood of the family descends. The relationship with the mother is broader. It includes not only the biological mother but stepmothers as well. As a child, I received the same kind of motherly care from all my father's wives, yet there were distinct differences when it came to the reality of the whole stratum of the family. The children of the same mother are known as a *cieng* (a household). The children of the same father identify themselves by referring to their biological mother.

Paternal uncles and aunts are part of the extended family. They are expected to respond to the demands of a brother's children and give them what they want or need, as their father would do. The paternal uncle has the same rights over the children as does their father, and it is he who must provide socially and economically for the child if the father dies. The bonds uniting the paternal cluster of relatives are thus very tight. The children are obligated to express equal respect for all senior members of the father-clan.

The position a woman occupies in the family is crucial to keeping the group together as a *cieng* (household). Like father, the concept of mother can also be understood in a collective sense. She is *man Naath* (mother of the nation) or the center of life and, like the paternal relatives, her brothers and sisters are respected and obeyed. However, the mother's brother may only claim rights over his sister's children if her husband fails to pay the bridewealth or dowry. Among the Nilotic people, it is very difficult for a woman to remain in a relationship with a man who has not fulfilled his marriage obligations. Among the Nilotic people, paying the bridewealth is like obtaining a marriage certificate from a local official in Western culture.

The wife subsequently strengthens her rights in the family by bearing children with her husband. At the same time, she strengthens her role as the center of life within her husband's family. (Prior to his marriage, the husband's mother served as his center.) The husband's family respects his wife's role and responsibilities, and she in turn must respect her husband and his relatives

5

Patrilineal descent, despite centering responsibility on the father, does not mean that the mother is powerless with regard to her own children or in family affairs. So long as she is alive, she is entitled to assist, advise, bless, or punish her children, especially if they scoff at her authority. Among the Nilotic people, a mother is the only one who will not curse her child. This is because she and the child have once shared the same life. This love is frequently expressed by the mother saying, "I gave life to this child."

It is the father's responsibility to protect and care for his family. However, if a father or a mother fail to care for their children, their kin provide necessities for them. The Nilotic people believe that giving birth to a child does not alone make a parent. Caring for and raising a child to adulthood are also included in the understanding and the responsibility of parenthood.

Marriage among the Nilotic society is a family responsibility; hence, any proposal has to be approved by both families. A young man or woman can only marry someone who does not share their father or mother's line of descent, because the Nilotic people are very much aware that marrying into the same bloodline is incest. They believe that those who commit incest cannot live, or if they do, their children will not live.

Divorce is rare among the Nilotic people, but it does occur. If a man fails to fulfill the bridewealth, he loses not only his wife, but also his rights over their children. When this happens, the woman and her children become the responsibility of her family until the children are grown enough to take care of themselves. The man who marries their mother can claim these children. He will have rights over the children as long as he cares for them.

The individual in the African orientation is viewed as a community creation and a community responsibility, as is well stated by the Yoruban proverb, "It takes a village to raise a child." This view is grounded in a presumption of equality of individuals within the society. One's existence begins on the day of birth. The young are taught and encouraged to act independently. Before assuming their role in the community, however, individuals must first be initiated and oriented into their new world, a world in which one observes and experiences countless ups and downs. Alongside one's kin, the growing child learns and acquires knowledge of what is accepted and what is not. Community solidarity is expressed in social obligations to help one another and to promote the common interest.

During a pregnancy, it is the parents who are responsible for the unborn child. The mother is given certain restrictions on diet and drink in order not to harm the baby. I remember very well that while I was pregnant with my first baby, my mother stayed with me to see that I ate the right foods. At that time, most of my diet came from fresh farm produce. Even when I came to the United States, I continued to be careful about what I ate, because I was nursing my fifth child. I did not eat pork until my son was two years old.

As the Nilotic child grows up, the family group shapes the child's destiny. For example, to make a baby strong, powerful, wise, and intelligent, the mother gives the baby a bath in various kinds of herbs and eats certain foods, particularly certain meats. She eats gazelle meat to make her child an untiring worker and cooperative in society. Consuming buffalo meat is considered to make the baby strong, wise, powerful, and a good leader.

A child is usually raised according to the family's expectations and will. Subsequently, one's success or failure is everyone's success or failure. The family influence ends only when the individual's life ends. The earthly community has no say in the life beyond the gates of death, yet the spirit of the departed remains to influence the family. These spirits are respected and honored so that they do not become angry and cause malaise in the family.

My husband Wal wrote his dissertation, *Neither Palaces nor Prisons,* about life among the Nuer (Duany 1992). He said that it is the individual's and the family's responsibility to keep ties of kinship. The lineage groups of the Nilotic groups perform important corporate functions in organizing marriage, exchanging cattle in marriage (bridewealth), aiding each other in the payment of bloodwealth (when a man is killed a certain amount of cattle is paid for compensation), settling disputes, and handling external conflicts by negotiation or armed combat. Genealogical relationships are defined in terms of rights and duties. In a society where the same customary rights and duties are observed by all members, a balanced exchange of goods and services between the kin on the father's side and the kin on the mother's side is maintained in certain important activities, including marriage.

Although feuding affects paternal as well as maternal kin, the paternal kin play a larger role. Paternal and maternal kin are from a different lineage, and therefore have a different network of relationships within which to address family affairs. Their common interest is the children born of the union in which they have a common descent. The husband or wife is not normally a party to decision-making processes in the other's territory, but they can help each other when it is necessary.

The well being of the community, as well as individual successes and failures, depends upon hard work and ancestral blessing. An inexplicable misfortune or epidemic is enough to make people speculate that the cause is the breaking of the covenant between human beings and the *Kouth*, the Creator. If someone wrongs the ancestors, then the Creator will be angry. To be restored to peace, health, and prosperity, the broken covenant must first be restored. The essential condition for restoration is recognition and confession of wrongdoing. Led by the elders of the families, community members come together and participate in making sacrifices such as killing a bull and feasting on its meat that is offered in seeking mercy, forgiveness and reconciliation.

The Cohesiveness of the Community

The family lineage descends from the father. It consists of all the segments of offspring from a single ancestor. Sometimes internal conflicts between segments arise, such as disagreements over family affairs or the use of common-pool resources, such as grazing land, fishing grounds, and water sources. However, there are always solutions. When relationships are disrupted because of mistrust and disharmony, one or more segments come together to mediate a reconciliation and establish a degree of forgiveness.

A community of cooperation is developed through the division of labor. The simplest divisions are among men, women, and children within a household. More complex divisions are apparent at the wider level of the community and the society. Such statements as, "You have to do your share. You have to learn how to get along with others," are common.

This level of family involvement and commitment may seem like interference to someone who is not African. But it functions as a social mechanism that keeps the larger family group integrated. Social solidarity, interaction, and the desire to maintain a general level of well being are seen as the responsibility of every member of all Nilotic communities. Given this emphasis on hanging or sticking together, everyone's foremost concern is each person's success. Everyone is equal, whether rich or poor. Each member is given plenty of encouragement and help in order to make their lineage a success.

The involvement and concern of a brother or a sister is far more respected than amassing wealth for personal use. The Nilotic groups are funded on a sharing formula that is expressed by the phrase. "When I have, we have, when I do not have, we do not have." This formula of "sharing" is the another foundation upon which the Nilotic groups are built. Because of this communal togetherness, it is impossible to find in the same community extremely wealthy or extremely poor people. Those who "have," my husband Wal said, assure the best standard of living for those who "have not" (Duany 1992). There are social rewards that motivate individuals who generously share. Thus, people work harder to have more and share more. They are motivated to do so because they gain respect or esteem in the community. In addition, they feel a moral obligation to share what they have acquired with others. Simply, sharing is the right thing to do. No one has so little that they cannot share something.

The well being of each member in the family is far more important than anything else, and no matter how troublesome it may be to find a solution to a problem. Life is togetherness. Among the Nilotic today, the people who leave the community to find work in towns or cities always send home money, clothing, and useful items to the members of their family who are less fortunate in villages.

This sharing formula is difficult for Westerners to understand. Soon after my family came to the United States, I arranged to bring my niece, Jam, from Sudan to live with me. At the time, we had very little money and lived in a small apartment. Some of my American friends could not understand why we were adding to our already overloaded responsibilities. To us, however, it was the right thing to do, because Jam would benefit from the opportunity to get an education. We all pulled together and today Jam is a college graduate and is helping her younger brothers and sisters.

This expectation of being communal is essentially the homogeneity and balance of the group, a group that always wants to see its members equal, but not identical. Accordingly, a member has no right to use another's goods at will. Each member is expected to undertake his or her share of the hard work. The person who makes no effort to improve, who sits waiting for others to help, will simply have a hard time in the community. Begging, when no personal effort is first attempted, is seen as shameful and humiliating. Only after unsuccessful efforts to care for oneself may kin become a community responsibility. There are no specialized welfare institutions that care for the disabled or elderly—the family and the community care for their members. Caring for each other is seen as part of the continuation of life. Older people care for the young, and the young will care for the elderly. This is expressed in the Dinka folk tale that my aunt used to tell me:

> Do you know why a fly eats only the rotten food? It is because a long time ago it neglected and mistreated its grandma and grandpa. It never provided food and water and the old flies died of starvation. The grandparents then cursed the fly. Since that time flies have had misfortune. They are to eat nasty food forever.

This story is told to every little girl and boy in Dinka country. Young people take this lesson seriously. Every young boy and girl wishes for success and the blessings of their elders.

Communal Life as the Goal of Existence

The fundamental goal of existence is life, both here and beyond death. Love, charity, forgiveness, good fellowship, and concern for one another are viewed as the basis for achieving a good society and are not only esteemed, but are greatly encouraged. These virtues are the sole path to real life. But as in any human society, evil exists in the form of hatred, anger, and resentment. Evil acts such as envy are discouraged among the Nilotic. If one does envy someone else for their child or wealth (cattle), that person is told not to do so because it could bring him

12

or her bad luck. Each person and the community as a whole strive to achieve a harmonious social life.

For example, to ease the burden of hard labor or heavy work, people join in small rotary groups known as *kaya* in Dinka. Young men from the villages work in each other's field. It is an effective method of providing services to everyone. When a family wants to build a *luak* (cattle barn), they invite the whole village to help. Women pool their resources to prepare meals and wine for the workers. Using total community mobilization, a *luak* that would take months to build is constructed in just a few days. "Strength lies in union" is an important value of Nilotic communities.

The Nilotic people are pastoralist. Their way of life is transhumant, that is, they move their cattle seasonally into areas where the herds will be certain to survive. The daily work of tending herds demands a great deal of labor from individuals. It requires communal effort where the central goal is survival. No one speaks of "my life" as being separate from "our life" *(cieng Naath)*. There is no other alternative in the Nilotic orientation. It is *Naath aa thin* (I am, because the community is). Without the community, my existence becomes meaningless. In other words, when there is community, I am; when there is not, I am not.

African theologian John Mbiti (1970) said it well:

> In traditional African life, the individual does not and cannot exist alone except corporately. An individual owes one's existence to other people, including those of past generations and one's contemporaries. One is simply a part of

13

the whole. The community must therefore make, create, or produce the individual; for the individual depends on the corporate group. Physical birth is not enough: the child must go through the rites of incorporation so that it becomes fully integrated into the entire society.

Without the community, the individual becomes meaningless. I taught my children this way. As an immigrant family living in the United States without relatives nearby, we have had to pull together to make our life meaningful in our new culture. Here my children have grown up missing the community of extended family I enjoyed when I was young. I miss waking up in the morning and hearing some old person singing in one of the huts or hearing another walking around the compound praying and greeting others with words of advice and encouragement. The circle around the fire always included most of our elders, who looked forward to teaching us young ones all year long. The circle seemed to grow larger each year as more children were born and became a part of the learning group.

Here in the United States, I find my family circle growing smaller instead of larger as my children leave for college and jobs in other communities. As I grow older, there will not be a larger circle as I experienced in Africa, but I will find my place in the smaller circles of my individual children's families.

The Importance of Personal Relationships

When spider webs unite, they can tie up an elephant. (Dinka Proverb)

My mother loved to tell spider stories. She believed that spiders are very intelligent little creatures. She always told my sisters and me to be smart in confronting life's issues. I also learned to tell stories to my children. I loved telling them the following story called Akarkar ku jala Adiel, The Spider and the Antelope.

In the savanna land, the story goes, it was a time of the year to burn the tall dry grass that had grown on the plains. This was when hunters gathered with their dogs to catch the game animals that tried to escape. One day the fire was spreading toward the place where the gray spider lived. He saw fire everywhere! How could he escape? He scurried as fast as he could to where the herd of antelopes was grazing.

"Please, friend antelope, don't leave me in this big trouble, I beg you. Carry me out of this fire. You have long legs. You can run faster than the hunters can. Quickly, let's flee to the forest."

The antelope was happy to help his friend. He told the spider, "Crawl into my ear and hold on tight. Here we go."

When the fire came near the Antelope jumped through the flames and sped into the forest with his friend, the spider, in his ear.

The spider was so grateful, "Thank you very much, my friend antelope," he said. "Someday when you are in trouble, I will be there when you need me."

Some days later, hunters came into the forest with their spears, bows and arrows, and dogs to catch animals. They hunted and hunted the whole forest until they found antelope tracks. The antelope tried to run away, but he knew the hunters and dogs were coming closer. Then the antelope saw his friend the spider.

"Please, friend Spider," he said, "can you help me today? If not, the dogs will catch me. Where can I hide?"

The spider answered, "My friend Antelope, speed is your strength, Run, I will stay in your tracks, I will hide you."

While the antelope ran deeper into the forest, the spider stayed to work in the antelope's tracks. After a while the hunters and their dogs came to the place where the spider had been working. They saw the antelope tracks. The tracks were covered with spider webs.

"We might as well take the dogs back to the village," The hunters said to each other. "These are old tracks. Look at all the spider webs."

So the hunters with their dogs went back to the village. The antelope lay down to rest deep in the forest. He was very tired from running so fast and long. His friend the spider had saved his life.

The lesson of this story is that all things are interconnected. People need one another.

The Nilotic believe that the world is full of endless ups and downs, and that people depend upon one another to get through them. This teaching went through my mind as I told the story to my children. Our family was safe in America, but so many of our people were suffering at home. *I will be there when you need me.* I came to realize that my homeland needed me to help in solving its problems. Though I am just one of so many southern Sudanese who would like to improve the conditions in our country, I believe that by contributing together we can make a difference. We have that responsibility.

My Personal Homeland

My homeland is the basin of Sobat River of southern Sudan. During my childhood, I was loved and secure. I was a participant and also a beneficiary of what people did to make the best use of their environment to provide for the necessities of life. I remember going to collect water at the well, going to the forest to collect firewood, milking cows, and doing all that a little Nilotic girl was supposed to do.

My mother had particular beliefs about the ways in which the future of her children were to be determined. She believed that a child had to drink a lot of milk, live in a well-structured environment, and learn the social customs and moral principles. She taught me that an individual is a part of a family. There is no fulfillment of one's duties or one's pleasures as an isolated individual. If a man is not a husband, and a father, then "he is nothing." A woman who is not a wife and mother is not a "real" woman. She is nothing. There are no old maids or old bachelors among the Nilotic people. Not marrying is not only a cause for shame, but also a sin against the will of *Kuoth* (the Creator), who has commanded every Nilotic to marry and beget offspring.

In my family, my father and mother played complementary roles. Their roles are recognized as the duality that comprises the union. Among the Nilotic, the woman of the house is the mother of the whole family, including her husband. She is the one who tends and feeds her family. When she offers food, she is offering her love, and she does so constantly. When her food is refused, it is as if her love was been rejected. I remember that at most meals, all of the children were fed first. My mother would hastily eat the leftovers as she worked.

All of the domestic responsibilities of the household were the domain of my mother. She was the one who directed and supervised the daily life of the household. She comforted the child who had been punished (not with spoken sympathy but with milk and a piece of sweet potato). She slapped hands for minor offenses. All members of the household depended on her vigilance to help them behave as good Nilotics in the daily routines of living. In my family, we knew that my mother was an efficient and skillful housekeeper, and that she sustained the harmony in our family. We children knew my mother as *man cieng*, the mistress of a "beautiful household." She was a real woman, her position unchallenged by anyone in the family, including my father. She was *mandiit*, the matriarch of her family and clan.

My family taught me that there are a host of rights and obligations between a parent and a child to which each refers explicitly and freely. Basic to all these, however, is the one which is seldom demonstrated verbally or physically. It is constantly invoked in absence and in respect: namely, parental love. My parents told their children "I love you" indirectly, never praised them to their faces, and seldom kissed them after they were four or five years old. But my parents loved us always, no matter what happened. Their love was always present. Sometimes my mother showed irritation, but I always believed in her unshakable love and care.

Nilotic mothers show their love in countless ways. A mother might pawn her beads and jewelry or go hungry in order to give her children the skills of life, both in traditional and modern ways. She might plead with authorities hostile to change, whether a Christian colonial government or an Islamic Arabic government, to win freedom for her children. She might trudge miles through the hot sun of sub-Saharan Africa. She might wait and keep faith while her daughters are far away in boarding schools or in an unknown land. Whatever she had to do, a Nilotic mother prepared her daughters to carry on the tradition of motherhood.

We children took the quality of our mother's affection so much for granted that any question about it came as a surprise. "She loves us, so even if we did hurt her, how could she be angry with us?" The love of Nilotic parents have for their children, sometimes labeled unbreakable by outsiders, is described by the mother as *gat jiec de*, the child of my womb. Aside from the crises that evoke heroic action, my parents' love was manifested through constant caring and solicitude about every aspect of the family. Love was manifest especially regarding the welfare of children, by asking, "Are they warm enough? Have they eaten enough? Who is sick?"

Naturally, then, we children expected our parents' support in preparing us for adult life. For my sisters and me, that preparation involved practical instruction in motherhood skills as well as our spiritual education. It also it included the marriage arrangement. When a daughter behaves well, the family is well regarded and respected in the community. Many young men will wish to marry into that family. This will bring a great amount of bridewealth into the family. The exchange of bridewealth creates important inter-group relationships and is also a mechanism for creating political and economic relationships. All these are a joy and pleasure to the parents.

Our parents were required by tradition to arrange a series of initiation ceremonies for my brothers. This began with the removal of the son's lower teeth at age ten, and ended with a marking ceremony at age fourteen or fifteen. This initiation was to prepare the young man to become a warrior. Since my brothers attended school, they did not go through these traditional ceremonies. Attending school determined whether one went back to the traditional way of life or whether one continued on to explore new ways of life. These obligations were to be fulfilled according to my parents' wishes, for the development of a child was to be a source of direct gratification for the parents. In an almost literal sense, what happened to the child happened to the parent. Our achievements in one way or another reflected honor on our parents, just as our failure or disgrace was a direct reflection of shame.

My mother often expressed her love through worrying. While my father worried as well, he did so in manly silence. My mother expressed her feelings openly. Worrying is not viewed as an excess, but rather as an expression of affection. The Nilotic people believe that if one worries actively enough, something good may come of it. One "worries out" bridewealth, or finding a good husband for a daughter, or a good and polite wife for a son. The intense worry of my mother was proof of her love. When one of us children was hurt, she cried to the spirit of her grandmothers: "*Maa oo!* Oh Mother! It should have happened to me instead of to my child!" She threw up her hands and then threw herself down to show her endless love. Even before anything happened, my mother would

20

worry about it. There was magic in her worry. It not only proved her love, but it kept misfortune away.

My Mother's Lineage

My mother, Atiel, was of *Ciec* Dinka. Her father was a famous and rich man, Machot Ayol Atany from the Yirol district in the Bahr el Ghazal region. He was a spear master (*Bany Bith*) and rainmaker, and a leader in his community. His knowledge of ecology made him an especially and well-respected man. He inherited his skills from his father, who was a rainmaker as well.

Among the Nilotic, height and strength are considered beautiful. In the village, my maternal grandfather was the young man most admired by all the young women. He had the most sex appeal. Many young women put down an admirer's looks by comparing his body to Machot's. "Who are you?" she would say. "I can't talk to you because you do not look like Machot."

Machot was also well known for his bravery. He was seven feet tall with a well-built, muscled body. He was a great dancer and singer, but many men of his age feared him because of his athletic ability. In wrestling, he was very strong. No one of his age ever put him down to his knees. Because he could run fast, no one could ever catch him. Machot was a very good hunter. When he was still a youth, he killed a lion with his bare hands.

How did Machot kill a lion with no spear or stick? This was a mystery pondered by many young people of Machot's age. He eventually told the story to his own children, because my mother told me about it when I was in my fourth year in elementary school.

21

One evening, she said, my grandfather had gone to a nearby village where he was courting a beautiful young woman. That woman later became his wife, my maternal grandmother, Aciek Ahou. Aciek was tall and slim. In those days, the unmarried Nilotic young people did not wear clothing. The shape of their bodies was easily noticed. A young woman's body and her looks were a theater to young men. The young men would talk about the breasts, legs, and backs of the young women they admired.

I remember very well, when I was in my second year in intermediate school, that I used to listen to the conversations of my older sister and her friends. They would talk about the young men they admired. They described every detail about the ways they found young men attractive: one man composed love songs, another treated his bull with care. One youth had a passion for life, another big muscles, or a beautiful smile. They laughed and covered their faces when they imagined themselves with the men they thought were ugly. If my mother overheard such talk, she scolded them for judging people by the outward appearance. She said, "God created every person. Maybe that not-so-good looking guy is really beautiful inside."

Anyway, it was getting late and my grandfather Machot was still in the village. Aciek's old grandmother told her to dismiss the young man because it was getting too dark. At night the wild animals would come out looking for prey. Machot would have preferred spending the night in the village, sitting and talking to Aciek. He was not afraid of wild animals, but they agreed to break up their conversation and he began the walk home.

As soon as he left the village he sensed that something was following him, but he did not know what it was. Nilotic young men are trained to understand the behavior of wild animals, especially lions and leopards. Machot stopped to figure out what was going on. He took a step, and heard something take two steps. He then understood who his companion was because a lion's steps are heavy. Machot continued walking and the lion began to increase its steps to catch up with him. When the lion was almost upon him, Machot suddenly stopped and the lion found itself too close to spring. The lion quickly turned to the side to prevent Machot from striking.

Machot knelt; he was wary and expecting the attack. The lion knew a fight was coming and jumped straight at Machot with no nonsense. Machot crossed his arms above his head to block the lion. When the lion hit Machot's strong arms, it fell on its back to the ground. Machot quickly followed the lion, not giving it a chance to get up. He then gave the lion a hard blow with his fist on the kidney, causing it to roar at top voice, "Hii rr-rr-rr-rrr." The animal struggled, partly stunned, its quivering tongue protruding from its mouth. The lion never roared again. Machot continued punching the lion in the kidney until it lay still. "It won't do to leave him so," thought Machot, "when he revives he'll be as dangerous as ever." He dealt the brute more blows, settling its fate.

When the people in the village heard the lion roar, they all grabbed their weapons and ran towards the sound, thinking that Machot had been killed by the lion. When they arrived, they found the lion dead and blood flowing from its mouth. Machot was singing this song to his bull lion, "*Mor koor! Tiit root, wen Ayol cin been.* Male lion! Watch out, son of Ayol is coming." Since that night, Machot's nickname became *Mony Koor* "The Lion Man." But he was known

23

among the young men as *Aguac Koor* "Mr. Lion's Fucker," a name the young women were embarrassed to call him. The lion's hide became a family treasure and was used by young men of his clan during dances.

The story also became a family treasure. When my family came to live in Indiana, I told my children this story. It became one of the favorites they used for show-and-tell in their classes.

My Father's Lineage

In our family, the spiritual and the intellectual were the realm of my father. He was a Nuer man called Bil Lual Machar. He was born in Waat, a small town in the Upper Nile Region, southwest of the Sobat River. His father, my grandfather, Lual Machar, came from the largest section of Lou Nuer called Gon. These people called themselves *Diel*, the original founders of the Nuer society.

Like my maternal grandfather, Lual Machar was a famous and rich man. He was well known and respected, even among the neighboring Nyarweng Dinka. He had many wives, both from the Nuer in the far west and from the Dinka in the south. Some of his wives were given to him in order to establish relations and build alliances between the Nuer and the Dinka.

He fathered many children, mostly daughters and only four sons. His daughters were married all over the Nuer country. Two of his sons died at infancy, but my grandfather Lual and his brother Nyanggol survived. They were from different wives.

My paternal grandmother was Dinka. She came from the large family of Deng Kuol of Nyarweng Dinka of Duk Padiit. Deng, the father of my grandmother, had many sons and few daughters. His

24

youngest son, Monyroor, was ready to marry but there were not enough cattle left for the bridewealth. He would only be able to settle his bridewealth when his younger sister married. There was no other way to get the cattle, so the family decided to take their daughter Akec to Nuer country to be married to a rich man. At age of eleven, Akec was taken to Nuer country, where her father Deng chose Machar's family.

Akec was a very beautiful young girl. My grandfather Lual, who already had three wives, was attracted to the young Akec. He told his father he would like to take the little girl as his fourth wife. My great-grandfather agreed to settle the marriage. The family offered to pay twenty-five head of cattle, but Lual asked his father to pay more because he liked the young girl. Fifteen head of cattle were added to make a total of forty. It was the highest bridewealth ever paid by a Nuer to marry a Dinka girl. My young grandmother Akec was then taken to the house of one of Lual's sisters to live until she became a woman.

At the age of fifteen, Akec had her first baby. He was named Bil, after one of the most beautiful bulls loved by Lual Machar's father, my great-grandfather. He had refused to give it for any marriage, only to be paid to Akec's father for a bridewealth. That was a very special honor for my great-grandfather, Deng.

Right after the birth of Bil, Akec died.

Deng died the same year. Monyroor, Akec's brother, felt he should return part of the bridewealth, but my grandfather Lual Machar refused. Lual said, "It was God's will that I lost my wife. I don't want any of the cattle back. I have the child, Bil. Let's all pray to God and to the spirit of his mother that they will be with him always."

Monyroor, as Akec's brother, offered to raise his little Nuer nephew. So Bil was taken to Dinka country and that is where he spent his childhood. Then, as today, ethnic identity is the strongest social identity among the Nilotic people. Every dry season, when the cattle are moved to the *toich* (flood plain), the grazing land, my grandfather Lual Machar would go to visit Bil in Duk Padiit. There he would teach Bil how to use weapons, fishing spears, and a fighting stick in the manner of a Nuer warrior. Father and son spend many days fishing and hunting together. My grandfather Lual Machar never believed that the Dinka people were good warriors.

At the age of six, Bil was taken back to live in Nuer country, but it did not work out well. My grandfather Lual spent most of his time arguing with his wives about Bil. He thought Bil was not receiving good care and that he was being made to do the work of the other young boys. Bil was required to look after young goats, sheep, and calves, but at age six, he really was too young for the job. Grandfather began to fear that he might lose Bil. He decided to send Bil back to live with his uncle Monyroor among the Dinka until he was old enough to care for himself.

While Bil was living in Dinka country, his father Lual died. Monyroor decided to keep Bil in his household. My father only returned again to Nuer country for his marking ceremony, when he was initiated to manhood at about age fourteen.

In 1963, when he was an old man, Monyroor came to live with my father. He told us the family history. He told us that after he had married again, he began having disagreements with his wives. They, like Lual's wives, were neglecting the orphaned Bil. He felt that had no choice but to send Bil to live at a mission

26

school run by Episcopal missionaries in the Malek Bor district. Monyroor said, "I had seen children without mothers who were being taken good care of by those foreigners. They did not have children of their own, but they treated the Nilotic children very well." The school itself was not considered important to Monyroor. His concern was in finding a place where Bil would be well cared for until the time when he could make a life of his own.

In those days, few people cared about schooling. When the authorities notified the chiefs that children were required to attend school, they often declined to send even their own children. They had no idea that a Western education could be useful. This was something that the Nilotic, especially the Nuer and the Dinka, realized very late. My great uncle Monyroor did not understand at the time that schooling would be the pathway to modern life for my father.

At the school, my father was the only Nuer boy living among the Dinka. He did not have many good experiences with the Dinka boys, as he was the frequent target of ethnic (Nuer-Dinka) persecution. Whenever the Nuer raided the Dinka country, Bil was attacked. However, Bil had been trained by his father as a real Nuer warrior. He took no nonsense from any Dinka boy and was not easily beaten. He eventually became the most feared boy in school. He could fight very well, because he was skilled in wrestling and in using any weapon, from spears to sticks.

When the missionaries became aware of the trouble Bil was having as the only Nuer among the Dinka, they made him a captain of the school. My father, who had been taught by his father to always tell the truth, quickly earned the trust of the missionaries. He showed ability for leadership, especially because of the conflict resolution skills that he displayed among the schoolboys. These skills are part of everyday Nuer life, so Bil picked them up naturally. The first step in Nuer conflict resolution is to uncover the real issues and bring the whole conflict into the open. The Dinka were more likely to act before they had obtained all of the facts. The British missionaries liked Bil's method and, as a result, trusted him more than any of the other schoolboys. He eventually was baptized and given the Christian name Benjamin. To this day, the Nuer and the Dinka have never learned how to pronounce this name. Those who tried would shorten it by combining his two names together to form Benbil. Others called him by his ox name, Machok Bek, as he was known among the Dinka. Every Nilotic male has an ox name. The name describes the appearance of the bull owned by that particular man. Machok Beck means a black and white bull with a white ring around each hoof.

After four years of schooling, my father graduated with high distinction and became one of the teachers in Dinka country. At the age of 17, he was chosen by the missionaries to go to the Lakes region, Yiorl district, to a village called Macuor. There he was to help start a new mission and a school under the supervision of Reverend Gill. There he met my mother, who was the daughter of the rainmaker, Machot Ayol.

My mother was the youngest of thirteen children of the same mother. Her father Machot Ayol had other wives and other children besides. Nilotic families are usually large, because a large family ensures economic welfare. The family is the workforce, a unit of production, because the members can pull together.

28

The missionaries, who wanted to evangelize the Ciec Dinka, had targeted Machot the rainmaker. Winning him as a convert meant that most of his people would also convert to Christianity. My grandfather resisted becoming a Christian. First of all, he did not believe in the white people's God. Second, he was a leader of his people, a position he inherited from his father. He refused to join this new religion because he believed that his ancestors would never forgive him if he turned from the old ways.

Despite Machot's resistance, the missionaries were able to convince him to allow his daughter to marry Benjamin Bil Lual. This was partly due to the influence of his sons, who were very much interested in acquiring the bridewealth cattle. My mother told me that she did not want to marry someone who lived far away from her family and who, on the top of that, was a Nuer, an enemy of the Dinka. One of my uncles told me that they were very angry with my mother when she told the family that she did not want to marry my father. My uncles did not consider her feelings to be an issue. They knew that Bil had cattle, that he was a hard-working man, and that he could take care of a family.

My mother did not have a strong case to present to her family. She had to accept the marriage. It was some comfort to her, however, that they promised to support her in the marriage. The family told her that they would be there for her if anything bad happened. The bridewealth was paid and the marriage was settled. My father paid my grandfather Machot Ayol seventy head of cattle. After the traditional celebrations, my mother was taken to the mission where my father had a house.

My parents' marriage symbolized reconciliation as it is done in Dinka country. Still, the *Ciec* Dinka did not want to join the church. For them, to join was to abandon their ancestors. Before the death of my grandfather Machot, his children never joined the church. It was only my mother who became a Christian through the influence of Bil, who was associated with the church.

Before she died, I asked my mother to tell me more about how she became a Christian. I asked her if she believed in her new religion. She gave me a long lecture. "The churches have changed," she said. "The people nowadays do not have spirit. Their religion is nothing but noise and show. You young people have lost the true religion." That may be true. The Nilotic are being converted everyday by different new Christian denominations. But my mother told me she would never lower herself to go to any new church. She goes only to the Episcopal Church of Archibald Shaw, where she says people enter into conversation with God Almighty to ask for mercy. She will have nothing to do with "those churches where people challenge God to give wealth."

Learning about the Other World

My parents were the first Nilotics in their region to learn about the other world. My mother moved away from her family to live with my father and start a new life. For my mother, life was hard. But life was good too. All she needed was to learn how to make it work for her. My parents understood that the community was made of families, and families of individuals, each representing a balance of complementary and interacting parts. The mission was, in a sense, a new community.

My mother first spent three weeks taking lessons from Reverend Arnold's wife, who spoke a little Dinka. Reverend Arnold was the head of the mission. My mother learned stories from the Bible and was then baptized. Her new name became Roda. This made the English missionaries very happy because they had fulfilled their mission. My parents were then remarried in the church to fulfill their duties as good Christians. These events were the cause of a big celebration in the mission.

In 1993, I went to Khartoum, Sudan, to do academic research. During that visit I had a conversation with my mother and other relatives who came to see me. We started talking about her experience with the missionaries. After she shared her baptism story, I asked my mother whether she knew what she was doing. She said, "Know what? I couldn't even remember my new name. The English women would be calling me, 'Roda, Ro—daa!' And I would sit there as if they were calling somebody else until someone finally had to reach out to touch me. Then I would jump up and say, 'Oh, you mean me!' The English women would keep saying, 'Roda. Roda, this is your name now.'"

My mother's new name meant nothing to her, but it meant a great deal to the missionaries. It was a solution to some of their problems. Because the Europeans had a hard time pronouncing the African names, they told the African people to select a name from the Bible. It did not cause the African people to abandon their names, and people frequently combined the European and the African names. That is how my parents got their Christian names, as did many

Africans who became Christians. Archibald Shaw, the first missionary among the Dinka, acknowledged the challenges of working with the highly conservative Dinka people. Shaw, who was able to move beyond stereotypes and develop reciprocal friendships among the Nilotic. He earned the ox name Machuor. Machuor is the color of a gray eagle found in Africa, and is the name given to a gray bull. The name also conveys strength and hard work.

Even though my mother accepted conversion to Christianity, she never believed some Bible stories, especially the story of Adam and Eve eating the forbidden fruit. She and other women with whom I talked shared their understanding of the story. They told me that Adam and Eve were young people who disobeyed their elder (God) who told them not to meet until they received the blessing from God. This interpretation of the story is close to the Dinka belief. Young women and men are guided by tradition not to have sex until they are first blessed by their elders. If one disobeys, misfortune may occur that could lead to not having children, or losing one's children in infancy.

My mother worked for the missionaries' wives, cleaning and learning how to cook European dishes. She even learned how to bake cookies. She also taught the English women how to prepare Dinka food. She was paid, and eventually accumulated some money. She earned £.S.10 a month (ten Sudanese pounds) and, of course, she learned how to count money. This was her first experience earning wages. She kept her money with her trusted friend, the wife of Reverend Arnold. Mrs. Arnold taught my mother a new way of life. My mother was not comfortable with her new way of life, however. She later came to appreciate that what she had learned was useful in caring for her own family. She learned about health and nutrition, which gave her an advantage over the other Dinka women of her age. My mother did not buy clothing because she was given free clothing by the missionaries. She was not used to wearing clothing everyday. She said, "My body was itching all over because of the clothing so I took them off. The English laughed and told me to put them back on."

One day, my mother was working in the yard with Mrs. Arnold, who decided to test whether or not my mother would remember how much money she was owed. "Roda, would you tell me how much money you have now?" she asked. My mother stopped what she was doing. She started counting her figures, *tok, rou, diak...*"one, two, three." She had been working for five months, and had not yet received any money from Mrs. Arnold. After finishing counting, she said, "Fifty Sudanese pounds, and last year's money was 100 pounds, so the total is 150 pounds." They both broke out in laughter. Mrs. Arnold was excited, thinking that my mother had learned how to count. The thing she did not understand was that my mother knew how to count cattle long before she started counting money.

My father, who was a teacher, was well paid. He received thirty Sudanese pounds a month. He used some of his money to buy cattle. In three years time, my parents acquired over a thousand head of cattle. My mother said, "It did not cost much to buy cattle. It only cost a pound and half to buy two calves or a steer at that time." Both my parents, after five years of work, had accumulated a lot of wealth, both in money and cattle. My uncles took care of my parents' cattle. What was really interesting was that my parents bought most of their cattle from the colonial tax collectors. The

Nilotic people never sell their cattle. They can be dying of starvation but would never think of selling their herds. For a Nilotic, life without cattle is meaningless. But, forced by the colonial administration to pay taxes, the people faced the very difficult decision to give up their animals.

My father did not believe in marrying only one wife. He believed that with all his wealth, he could afford to care for a large family. He decided to marry his second wife. This brought about conflict between him and the missionaries who were his guardians. He did not listen to them, and went ahead and married to his second wife, who was from the Agar Dinka. He eventually married a total of five wives. The church would recognize only his first wife, my mother, as his legitimate wife. Her children were baptized and had rights in the church. My father's other wives and their children were not recognized by the church as being a part of my father's household. They were allowed to join the church on their own. This made my father very angry and he left teaching to start his own business. He opened a retail shop, where he bought local commodities and resold them to the people. His business grew, and he was able to open eight more branches in different villages.

From a small retail shopkeeper, he became one of the big wholesale merchants in the area. In 1955, he had a big store built, the first ever brick building in the area. Over years it became the center of activity in town. Everyday customers sat in the shade under mango trees in front of the shop. People wanted their bicycles repaired. Customers could find every type of merchandise: tobacco, dates, clothes, shoes, salt, sugar, onions, cooking oil, and kerosene. Anything not visible had to be ordered on the next trip my father took to the bigger town of Wau. The community in Akot became familiar enough to feel that they belonged to the store and the store belonged to them. My father and the people were locked up in the search for goods to buy and sell, which gradually contributed to social change among the Dinka people.

The shade behind my father's store gave a soft, make-believe feeling to our world. We children would play games there. Some would pretend to be the storekeeper and some would be village people coming to sell their produce. When my father's store opened in the morning, we could smell the mixed odors of onions and kerosene. The smell did not disturb us, but would disturb many Dinka people who were not used to such odors. We would laugh when we saw them holding their noses and turning away from the odors—some spitting and nearly throwing up.

Every day the store was full of laughter, jokes, bragging, and boasting. It was also place where the news of the day could be heard—who was going to court today or what happened to the case yesterday. Most of these court sessions were conducted under a big *cuei* tree, a tree that bore fruit as sour and sharp as lemon juice. When children sucked it, they would clench their teeth as if they had tasted something bad.

My father was the only Southerner who made a living as a businessman in Agar Dinka country. Not only did he teach the Agar Dinka new ways of life, but he also made them understand that there were new ideas that people could be useful. Since he allowed his children to attend schools, he influenced the Agar chiefs to allow their own children to attend school as well.

Before my father's death, I enjoyed listening to my parents' conversations. They would talk about their life in the mission, about what the missionaries had done well, and how they had changed the Dinka culture. Up to the time he died, my father would always joke with my mother, asking her why she did not want to marry him. And jokingly, he would tell my mother, "Now go! You are free. Go find somebody else to marry." My mother, who knew her rights—the right of being a mother—would say, "I am not going anywhere until you put all these children back into my womb. These children are my beauties, they are my whole life and my life is here. I'm not going anywhere, we are stuck forever."

My mother's words of advice have been my strength in my own marriage. I learned from her that divorce is not a solution to marital disagreements, and marriage is not a romantic institution. It is a social reproductive unit, an essential institution to the Nilotic people. The culture of which I am a part does not see women as just housewives, but as the center of their social reproductive unit. This unit is the center of a network that forms the political alliances of the Nilotic people.

Women are the center of life.

My mother
*Roda Atiel Machot Ayol
with my son Kueth*

Chapter II

Life Together

The self is formed relationally through social interactions. Culture provides the parameters for social interactions and at the same time is modified through social interactions. Our identities are constituted within the parameters of culture. In many ways, our identities are narratives told about ourselves as objects of our own past, present, and future.

Growing Up

Akot, where I grew up, is thirty miles east of the town of Rumbek. Akot is considered a small town, with about five thousand people scattered about. It is considered a town because it has a police station, a church, a school, and a number of small retail shops. The shops were owned by Arab traders. My father's shop was the only one owned by a Southerner from among the Nilotic people.

In Akot, people lived together with a sense of community. They would sit outside and talk with their neighbors, children would play and climb the trees. When someone got sick, neighbors would rush to help. Neighbors also shared things. Our neighbors would come to our house to chat with my mother, or to borrow a cup of sugar or a couple spoonfuls of salt, or to tell my mother their problems. Akot never failed to take care of its people. This was not a matter of opinion; it was faith. On the day that the people of Akot stopped believing, Akot lost its life as a community. Those people of Akot that kept the faith, like my parents, raised cattle and kept the old ways of life. However, they were open to change.

Indeed, the traditional Nilotic way of life was changing across the board. The colonial government was putting pressure on the chiefs to send their children to school. It was a new thing for parents to send their sons to school. This new obligation of attending school created an added incentive to spur boys to success. Girls did not begin attending missionary schools until the early 1950s. Even then, few girls actually went to school. There were fears among the Nilotic people that school would turn the girls into devils who lured men away from the right path. For example, when the Nilotic people saw the missionary husbands going into the kitchen to help their wives, they were shocked. Nilotic men did not help with women's chores, but rather kept the cattle and did the hard work.

My parents were pioneers in their approach to modern ways. Although open to change, they did not allow their children to neglect the traditions. In Nilotic society there is no other norm that claims stronger standing than a child's obligation to obey and respect his or her parents. My mother reminded me of this everyday. As a child, I came to learn the deference that I must show it to any older person, but above all to my parents. Respect was something that my parents never needed to ask for. I have never seen any of my older brothers or sisters challenge any adult, let alone our parents.

"If a child is disgraced, the parents are disgraced as well," my mother would say. From the time the girl begins to menstruate until the time her parents turn her over to her husband, her mother is responsible for her moral guidance. That's why mothers had to be very strict with their daughters and not make any mistakes. The burden of keeping the girls out of mischief weighs more heavily upon the mother than upon the father.

My sister Nyanalath was a fun-loving girl, but sometimes her ideas got us into real trouble. One day she played a trick on an old lady named Achok Nguan. Achok Nguan was well known in the town. She routinely came and asked for tobacco in my father's shop. When she came for tobacco, she would stop and talk with the children before entering the fenced yard to speak with our mothers. She would sing and dance and we would join her. Everybody in town knew her as Achokdit. Everybody liked her because she was so good with children. Mon Makat, Achok's husband, was a school carpenter. The couple did not have children. But it was not a problem for Achok, because all of the children in the community belonged to her. Sometimes my mother would send my sister and me to help Achokdit when she was sick. We fetched water and cleaned her yard and my mother would cook for her.

On the day of the trick, my sister Nyanalath and I went to play under a mango tree after finishing our duties. Along came Achokdit as usual to ask for tobacco.

"There is Achokdit," Nyanalath said. "I am going to teach her a lesson today."

"Why?" I asked. I didn't know what had gotten into my sister's head.

"Because I am tired of seeing her here everyday, asking '*tab, tab* (tobacco, tobacco).'"

Nyanalath went to the shop and got some tobacco. I was curious to discover what she was up to. She called to the old lady, "*Achokdit tab akin*, (Achokdit, here is the tobacco)." Achok happily took the tobacco and started putting it in her smoking pot. She was praising God and giving us blessings. After she prepared her smoking pot, Achokdit went to the fenced yard to light her smoking pot from the fire our mothers had made for cooking.

As soon as she began smoking, hot smoke full of chili pepper filled her throat and she started coughing violently. She coughed and coughed until she fainted and fell down. This attack took everyone by surprise. There on the ground lay Achokdit. Our mothers ran to where she fell. My sister and I could hear people calling out, "*Achokdit, Achokdit ee nguu*? Achokdit, Achokdit, what is wrong?"

We ran to see what was going on. My sister and I made a little hole in the fence and peeped through. The fence was made of grass, so it was easy for us to make a little hole and watch the drama we had created. I did not know what was in the tobacco. "What did you give her?" I asked.

"Nothing. Just a piece of tobacco."

"Just a piece of tobacco?" I repeated. Nyanalath surely was not telling me the truth.

When we saw Achokdit lying on the ground, we thought she was dead. We could see my mother running, carrying a jar of cold water. She poured it on Achokdit's head. When we saw that, we started running. We ran to a house across the road and stayed there until dark. We did not witness what happened in the yard after my mother poured cold water on Achokdit.

Achokdit spent a few more minutes on the ground. When she got up, she told the whole story to my mother. "Aker and Nyanalath gave me tobacco mixed with chili, and that's what caused me to cough." My mother took Achokdit to the clinic for check up. She was released and went home.

Nyanalath and I worried all day. We didn't know whether Achokdit had gotten up or was still lying on the ground. As it began to get dark, I became frightened and began asking my sister how long we were going to stay away from home. She told me that we would wait until dark and then sneak in without our mothers seeing us. I lost patience. "We have to go now," I said. "There is nothing we can do to stop what you did." I began walking towards our house. She had no choice but to follow.

Going home was one of the worst experiences I ever had. It was close to 7:00 p.m. when we sneaked through the fence, thinking nobody would see us. Everyone in our family knew what had happened. Our brothers and sisters all knew we were in big trouble, but they had been told not to tell us. We crept to our room to sleep.

My mother came in. She said, "I know both of you are in here. All I want to tell you both is that Achokdit is still in the clinic. We do not know what will happen to her. Your father and I have been waiting until you two came home to let you know that if Achokdit dies, you will have to bury her." She walked out and closed the door behind her. My mother knew that Achokdit was now resting at home.

I started crying, calling to my mother, and telling her that the whole idea was a mistake, that we did not mean to give her chili. "We're sorry. We won't do it again, " I pleaded.

My mother replied. "You are lying tonight, but tomorrow when you see her dead body, you will tell us what really happened. Now, go to sleep."

That night we were not given food because the family had eaten dinner while we were still hiding. We spent the whole night with no food. I could feel my stomach burning as if it were on fire. My intestines were making funny noises. My sisters who were not in trouble were laughing at us. It was a fun night for those who had not played a trick on Achokdit, but for Nyanalath and me, it was our night in hell.

Our real torment, however, was not the hunger we felt or the taunts we endured, but not knowing the old lady's condition. Was she dead? Was she well? These questions ran through my mind all night. We did not know the answers because nobody would tell us, not even the littlest ones in the family. When I finally fell asleep, I had nightmares. I could see Achokdit lying on the ground near the fire where she fainted. I could hear my mother's voice, calling, "*Achok, Achok ee gu*? Achok what is it?" I would snap out of sleep, only to find myself in the darkness of our room. The whole episode played in my mind as if Achokdit never got up.

In the early morning, around 6:00 a.m., Nyanalath and I were the first children to wake up. My mother was already waiting nearby to keep an eye on us. I started to open the door, but Nyanalath told me not to go out. She was thinking that we should go into hiding again. I said, "I am done with you." My big worry was seeing the dead body. I had never seen a dead body before. Among the Nilotic people, children are not allowed to go near the dead. This is because the Nilotic people believe that children do not understand why people die and it is better to let them learn when they are adults.

I opened the door slightly, took a deep breath, and walked straight to my mother who was cooking *legemat* (donuts). She pretended not to see me. I told her that we were sorry and would not do it again. I was holding my head with both hands, my nose was running, and my eyes were full of tears. Without looking at me, she told me to go back into the room until she was finished cooking. I tried to give reasons why I should stay, but my mother said, "I do not want to hear a word or whose idea it was. When I am finished, I will take you to where Achokdit is."

"*Nhalicdit piir!* Good Lord of Life," I said to myself, "What has happened to Achokdit?"

I wanted very much to convince my mother that the idea was not mine, but I didn't know how. Embarrassment and shame came over me like bitter cold. I felt dizzy, as if my blood vessels were jumping. I knew my mother very well. She did not play games when it came to disciplining naughty children. I went back to the room shaking like a puppy that had been thrown into cold water. My mouth danced as if my jaw did not belong to my head. My teeth made a noisy "kee, kee, kee, kee, kee, kee" that I had not heard before in my life. I tried to hold my mouth tight but the rhythm would not stop.

I walked in and my sister asked, "What did she say?" I gave her a look, climbed on my bed, and pulled the blanket over me. The guilt of harming the old lady was so intense that I wanted the earth to swallow me up before I could see Achokdit again. Eventually the door opened. My mother walked in and said, "Aker and Nyanalath, come out." I was sure that it was the end of my life. My heart was beating so fast that I thought it was going to jump out of my chest.

We felt stripped naked and walked like dogs who have lost their tails. Our heads were bent down. We looked out from the corners of our eyes. I saw my father standing near, silently watching us. This was a clear message that we were bad children. I thought I could never forgive myself for commiting such an act. We followed my mother to her hut. She told us to sit down, which we did without delay. Her first question was where did we get the tobacco. My sister quickly said, "From the shop." That admission in itself was a big mistake, because we were not allowed to go into the shop.

As my mother pulled out her whip, we both started begging, "We will not do it again!" She opened her eyes wide, and held the whip above our heads. We were shaking our heads and saying, "No! no! We will never do it again."

My mother asked, "Would you like for other children to do the same to me?"

"Oh, no," we responded, while quickly shaking our heads from left to right. She lowered the whip and said, "*Ting ke nhiim, eeke ci ciet diar jak*, Look at their heads—shaking like female magicians full of spirits."

Years later I thought about our shaking heads during my fist visit to a Pentecostal church service. It was a very lively service, with loud music and everyone shaking their heads and praying out loud all at the same time. It seemed my mother was very much correct in her metaphor, because Nyanalath and I had shaken our heads like people I saw praying in the Pentecostal church.

Thank God my mother did not whip us too badly that day. But a whipping is a whipping, and even a little can be very painful. The whipping took place in the morning around 10:00 a.m. In all, our torment had lasted a day and a half. The psychological and physical punishment taught a lesson we never forgot. From that day forward, no child in our family behaved badly. Our big lesson was to be respectful to everyone, not only to our parents but to others as well.

Still, my brothers, sisters, and I also had our good times. I remember a night when one of our brothers was stung by a scorpion. We were all sitting on the ground on a *yiig* (a mat made of papyrus) one warm night telling stories and making jokes. My two brothers started pushing each other back and forth. One brother shoved the other off the *yiik*, causing him to land on his back on the ground. We hadn't seen the scorpion, but as soon as my brother hit the ground, it went into action. My brother was stung close to his tail bone, and gave the loudest cry of his life. It was the loudest human cry I had ever heard. We all jumped to our feet. My father came to find out what was the matter. He immediately sent for the scorpion medicine-man. The scorpion-man came and gave my brother some medicine to chew. He also rubbed medicine on his buttocks. My brother spent the whole night crying in pain, but not as loudly as he had when he first got the sting.

Children are a Gift from God

According to the Nilotic culture, children are a gift from *Kouth*, (God) to their parents. Life ultimately is a gift from God. Children are always wanted in the Nilotic family because no adult is whole without children. Aside from traditional and social reasons, children are welcomed for the joy they bring to the family beyond gratification to the parents. The pleasure of having a child in the house is a gift of happiness for life. A house without children is a gloomy place. No children in the house means no brightness in the house. It is good to have children, because they show that God has blessed that marriage.

After the birth of first child, parents are re-named after the first born. For example, *man* or *guan* Aker (mother or father of Aker). Now I am called by my husband's family *Man* Duany (Duany's mother), after our oldest son Duany Duany. Children also gain honor by being called *Nya* for female or *Gat* for male.

The child who comes to bless a household is regarded as an individual from the moment of conception. Human souls were created by God when he made the universe. No parent ever forgets that the child is his or her own flesh and blood. From the time this child emerges from the womb into the open world, the parents have the full responsibility of making that child whole. The children then learn their duties of knowing and respecting their parents.

From the very youngest up to the oldest child, my mother and father enjoyed this respect. When I saw my father coming home from the shop or from the farm, I helped him by taking his shoes, giving him water, and doing anything else that would make him comfortable.

We obeyed my parents primarily out of respect, not fear. Among the Nilotic, a child is never terrorized at home. When the children were noisy, he had only to open his eyes and look at the child. There was a sort of lightning in his eyes. But "the look" is not intended to threaten; it was only a reminder to behave well and keep quiet because good children respect and listen to their parents. I remember when my father or any other adult was taking a nap, we would all try to be good, quiet children. The respect that surrounds parents extends to their possessions, even when they are not present. Mother's cooking pot and Father's fishing spear are all part of them and therefore earn the respect of their children.

On the other hand, fear was a possibility. Among the Nilotic people, both parents responded to any offenses. They administered appropriate punishment. They punished children chiefly for some infraction of the moral or social code, especially if the culprit had shamed the family in the eyes of the community, as my sister and I did when we played the trick on Ackodit.

When my mother whipped us that time, we did not struggle to free ourselves because we accepted our wrongdoing. We considered the whipping justified. My father told us, "You should be thankful to your mother, who just whips you. I am in a position to kill you two." Nilotic parents did for the good of their children. There was no such thing as drug addiction or alcoholism, which could cause a child to be mistreated. In my family, we never criticized our parents' actions. We expected them to know what they were doing.

My mother was the parent, beginning at birth, who spent more time with us children. Her punishments were frequent, ranging from slapping to major whipping, according to the level of misbehavior. Compliance in the family was encouraged by sanctions, most of which invoked the anxiety/conformity/approval syndrome, but methods could vary considerably according to the situation. In the Nilotic society, domestic duties, such as sending a girl to fetch firewood or water or sending a boy to tend the cattle, are used to punish non-conformists. These minor punishments came easily and were easily forgotten. Major punishment came less frequently and was long remembered.

We children, especially the girls, were under a deep obligation not to shame our parents. Children would say, "If I did such a thing, my parents would kill me." Pregnancy before marriage and laziness were things that shamed your family. "What have I done that God should punish me with such a child?" would be the outcry of parents who felt disgraced by the behavior of their daughter. People in the community would pick up on whatever the child did that was wrong and verbalize it as the disgrace of the parents.

Parental vulnerability was a sort of weapon. My parents' suffering served not only as a rebuke for the past, but also as a means to control the future. A child would say, "If I do not do (whatever), I will bring shame on them." Any or all misfortune can be traced by parents to troubles from the children. Yet children are perceived as a source of peace and stability for the family.

Parental sacrifice and solicitude pile up as a monument to parental love, the dimensions of which define the vastness of children's indebtedness. The shining reward that parents expect for all their care and sacrifice is the respect of their children and the knowledge that God has blessed them with children who will listen to their advice. Sometimes I feel that the translation into English is hardly adequate to express this deep gratification and exaltation.

Now, as an adult, I can understand why I am proud to be a Nilotic woman and a mother, but it is very difficult to be a Nilotic woman and mother. Parents sacrifice their whole lives to raising their children to be better people. Parenthood is a joy. When a child does well, there will be a long succession of blessings, including health, long life, and the parents' wish for grandchildren. If a child does wrong or fails to make good, the devoted parents are robbed of their meaning. A frequent, angry reproach by parents to a child that has done wrong is, "This child has no respect for us."

Through the child's success, the parents are validated, just as through defects the parents are disgraced and condemned. Therefore, through bonds of esteem, affection, and love, the fate of the parents and the child is inseparable.

Children are to respect and support their aged parents. The material part of this obligation involves providing for the daily basic needs of the elderly parents. When the child is successful, the parents boast proudly, "My children do everything for me. They look after me like their own eyes." Nilotic people teach their children that they are their parents' flesh and blood, and therefore no substitute for them is conceivable.

Given the very real differences in African women's material environment, their role expectations are profoundly different from Western women. Children are valued for social and economic reasons. A woman's role as a mother defines her identity in Nilotic society. The Nilotic people believe a woman with children makes less trouble for her husband. Through giving birth, women achieve social acceptance and security. Nilotic young women realize that children are their major source of prestige, influence, and long term security. Infertility is viewed by the society, and by infertile women themselves, as a personal failure and is often grounds for divorce. One of my father's wives divorced him because she could not have children. She initiated the divorce because she was not happy. It was difficult for my father to let her go, because she was a very nice lady.

In my family, a favorite phrase was "*Mal mu gua or yin apuol goup*, or the great peace of the household." Our house was always full of activity. The adults were busy taking care of the young. The children and babies were all busy growing up, enjoying life or suffering together. Although we grew up in the Dinka country, this Nuer phrase never left my father's tongue.

Mal (peace) was an important word in my family, and an important Nilotic concept. The root of the Nuer word *mal* means peace, health, and unbroken wholeness. It is like the togetherness of the mother and her baby in the womb. They both feed from the same blood vessels and that gives them the same heartbeat. When something goes wrong, both the mother and the child are endangered. A Nilotic household is like that. When there is something wrong within the structure, it must be fixed. That was my parents' duty. We children knew our parents as the repairers of the social fabric.

Family violence and quarreling were not considered the way of life in our home. "The Nuer do not fight each other," my father would say. When there was a dispute in the family, it had to be resolved right away, because to let it go on was a disgrace. However, if someone got into a fight at the playground and ran home crying, my father would say, "Go back. Nuer never give up to anyone." As an adult, I began to understand why the Dinka people did not like to fight the Nuer people. My mother told me that it was because the Nuer never stopped fighting until they defeated you. That is why the Nuer fight to the end.

My parents used to say that there would be peace in the world outside, if there were peace in the family.

The most common daily greeting in the Nuer family is "*mal puony du,* is your body at peace?" In the household, *mal* (peace) invokes unity. Peace in my family might be described more as a state of dynamic equilibrium, where each one knew his or her obligations and duties and where everyone was busy. Sometimes there might be an argument among the co-wives or children, but my parents were there to see that things were set right. All this was part of being a unit, showing one's affection and interest, and sharing in the experiences of one's family.

This concept of *mal* (peace) is sometimes difficult to grasp for those who were not reared in a Nuer family. Every problem in the family, as in the community, was subject to lengthy discussion. My father used to tell us that my mother, who was a Dinka, would quarrel with him because the discussions on family matters took too long. Peace, discussion, and disagreement were all part of life. Disagreement meant that someone had no peace. Discussions restored peace. Arguments were acceptable and, until the boiling point was reached, *mal* was not jeopardized. When someone was not at peace, they always jeopardized someone else's *mal*.

Human relations were expected to endure. There was seldom a final end to anything. My brothers were always my brothers and my sisters were always my sisters. Nothing so strongly demonstrates the sense of family cohesion as the help from relatives. Sometimes there are misunderstandings, but in times of crisis, our family hangs together and cares for our own. This mechanism is one of social justice within the family circle. It derives its force from the understanding that all are part of one integrated whole. This was the way my family's mutual obligations worked out. The mutual obligations acted almost as a form of insurance for the welfare of family members.

A Time to Remember

It was in this a warm human environment that I spent the first six years of my life. I had much attention, discipline, love, caring, play, and work. In short, I grew up totally immersed in a group where my own place was clearly defined. This arrangement I accepted as a given, for there was nothing peculiar or particularly noteworthy about it. It was how things were in this world among the Nilotic people of southern Sudan. I was happy and loved; my world safe and secure.

During the day our small town Akot was a mystery-filled expanse, awaiting discovery. There were things for children to seek, to do, to make, or to eat. There were things forbidden or things dangerous, according to whatever our imaginations cooked up.

I have many fond memories of visits to my aunts' and uncles' homes. As far back as I can remember, there has always been a place to which I belonged with a certainty that it could never be taken from me. When I say "home", I mean the group of people with whom I am connected and to whom I belong, the Nilotic people of southern Sudan. This is the reality in my life no matter where I am.

One time my mother and I went to visit my aunt Apuol in the nearby village call Pagrau in Yirol district. We arrived in the evening. I loved this aunt because she doted over me. Because I was so tall and slim, she would say, "This child is not getting enough to eat in school. Other children look good, but she is always so thin." She fed me all kinds of food, peanuts, sesame butter, yams, sweet potatoes, milk, and butter.

In the morning I followed my cousins to the river and saw all the village children laughing, shouting, and singing. Girls held their arms as if they were carrying a baby. They sang and when they finished they threw themselves into the water. *"Manh dia*, My Baby" is the song the girls sang when they were playing in the river:

> *Manh dia* My baby
> *Mor aci la gor pieu* Mother has gone to
> fetch water
> *Mor aci la kuany tiim ke mac*Mother
> has gone to fetch firewood
> *Manh dhia*My baby
> *Biet de eman* Be quiet now
> *Mor akin aci ben*Mother is here

I wanted to join them but I was afraid. I turned around quickly and pushed through crowds of women who had come to fetch water. I ran to my aunt's hut.

"Why are you back so early?" asked my aunt.

"No reason," I replied. But the truth was that I was afraid of the other children. I did not know them very well. I was wearing a very nice dress and thought they might take my dress and push me into the river and I might drown. After spending a few days in the village, I made friends with the children and began to trust them.

Another time I told my aunt Apoul that she the way she did her bead work was very intelligent. She said, "Intelligence is shown not only in reading and writing, but in whatever you do at your best."

My father had thirty-two children from five wives. All of his children attended school. Barnaba Marial, George Maker, Edward Ater, Andrew Laat, Ruben Marial, Eliah Matuany, and I attended universities. I am the only female in my family who has attended college.

I am the fourth of five children from my mother; all of whom survived to adulthood, I am the youngest of the three daughters. We all, except my oldest sister Akukuek (Mary) who has a disability, attended school. Akukuek caught a childhood disease when she was an infant and lost her hearing. My mother told us that Akukuek became very sick and would have died if not for modern medicine. We younger children later had the opportunity to be vaccinated against the disease.

My older brother Barnaba Marial became a medical doctor. My other sister Apanda (Martha) eventually dropped out of school. I became a schoolteacher. My younger brother Makuac (Augustine) joined the liberation movement after finishing high school. In 1989, he was killed by the Sudan People's Liberation Army/Movement (SPLA/M). According to the story I was told, Makuac had a disagreement with his commander, resulting in his murder.

The intricate ways in which relationships are drawn among the Nilotic people make it almost impossible for an individual to become destitute. Not having connections with another living soul is just unimaginable. One could conceivably be minus parents, or have neither spouse nor sibling, but to be alone with no living relative, with no one to care for or to lean on, is virtually unheard of.

The adults in my world no doubt had their happiness and their sorrows. But childhood, by its very nature, is a magic-filled world, wonderfully carefree, innocent, and happy. My childhood was all these things and more, in a world full of trusted adults. In my mind, the distinction was not important. My mother was also a mother to all of my father's children. My father's four other wives were also my mothers. At any of their houses I was fed, washed, and my hair braided. I accepted, without question, that all of them were my mothers and their homes were mine. Thus, I spent the earliest years of my life in a world filled with a real, immediate, and tangible sense of belonging. I was wanted, loved, and cherished.

Though the days had their own treasures, it was the nights that brought the whole family together in a magic circle as prelude to refreshing, restoring, restful sleep. Night was heralded by the livestock—chickens, goats, sheep, and cattle—shepherded into their various enclosures and *luak* (cattle barn).

The responsibility for each of these groups of animals was allocated to specific individuals, and mostly fell on the young boys and girls. The adults assumed the primary role of directing and overseeing, followed by the older children. They had the right to monitor everything and assure that their knowledge and skill were passed on to the next generation. As soon as a child could walk and talk, the child was given tasks to perform. In the beginning, those tasks were simply helping someone else. In this way the child learned to sweep, carry water from the well or river, milk cows, fetch firewood, stoke the fire, and grind or stamp *dura* (sorghum) or grain. These were some of the first tasks I learned. Girls and young boys milk cows, goats, and sheep, feed the young calves, and herd the livestock. The older boys also learn hunting and fishing. I didn't know it, but my time of learning in the village with other little Nilotic girls was to be cut short by the new tasks of learning to read and write.

After the livestock were safely in their places, the evening meal was cooked and cows were milked. The grandparents were busy with the youngest children, who had a hard time staying awake. The grown-ups busied themselves with evening chores, including putting out *yiik*, the weed mats, or *bok*, the animal skins, upon which people sleep. The sleeping arrangements were prepared ahead of time, because after the babies were fed, they were put to bed.

Among the Nilotic people, a child is considered proof of female accomplishment rather than a burden. I remember my mother doing work while carrying my little brother on her back. The image of the African woman carrying a heavy head-load and a baby on her back may be somewhat disconcerting to Westerners, but carrying a baby and feeding it while engaged in other activities is ordinary activity for Nilotic women. Life among the Nilotic people requires a high level of physical effort, so it is not easy to draw a line between hard work and too much work.

By age of two, I was taken to the cattle camp. I had a baby sister and, by definition, was no longer a baby. Thus I was qualified to sit around the evening fire with the other children, waiting for the evening meal and listening to stories. This was a time when the elders shared their life stories and gave advice to the young. The purpose of sitting around the fire was to teach children, to develop shared experiences, and and to solve problems. The conversation differed from person to person and from day to day.

What mattered in this time of teaching was the specific meaning in a person's life at a given moment of time and place. Each situation in life represented a challenge and presented a problem for one to solve. Understanding the meaning of life was everybody's task, and each life-lesson was unique, as was each specific opportunity to express it. When an adult taught from his or her life experience, the message was always clear and carried moral weight. Each individual was responsible for reflecting upon the reality of his or her experience, and from that experience, coming to an understanding the meaning of life.

One of my first lessons as a child was learning to listen. This was my uncle's favorite song, and my mother used to sing it to my children too. "*Pingke wee miith thikor,* Listen You Little Ones:"

*Ping ke wee miith thikor*Listen you our little ones
Wun kuon diit adai The ancestors are watching
Wun kuon diit alang The ancestors are praying
Akol ku pir aa wek The time and life is you
*Ping ke wee miith thikor*Listen you our little ones

As I said before, the stories told around the fire were meant to teach the children something about life. We loved listening to the adults tell about ogres and giants, animals of the forest, great beasts, or little hopping creatures of the world. I remember terrifying tales about creatures of the great River Nile, huge scale covered crocodiles that could crush people and animals to death and swallow them whole. Later, when they were hungry again, the crocodiles could bring them up and swallow them again. We children listened to every word and believed. These stories were told with such vivid detail and with such vocal expression that we saw them in our minds and lived them in our feelings. How we cried when told the tale of a little orphan girl or boy who was on the way to help an uncle or grandparent, but fell into the hands of an ogre disguised as a kind little old lady, who tried to eat the child for dinner.

Some stories filled us with laughter, especially when cruel giants or cannibals came to grief, usually by falling prey to the own traps intended for their victims. There of course were inspiring tales of powerful and brave men and women; stories that gave us heroes.

The faces around me on those nights as a child in the cattle camp were smiles with eyes sparkling like stars on a moonless night.

In summer, when the cattle were moved to the *toich* (flood plain), the days stretched endlessly. I will forever remember laughter, inspired by the birth of a new, colorful day warmed with the African tropical sun. The songs of the morning are godlike rhythms, bringing memories to every soul aspiring to pray for the ancestors.

Cattle camps offered space to play and to roam. There, the children could run and run with no fence to bound and still remain in clear view of the adults. I remember how good it felt to run barefoot and feel the grass massage my feet. But on rainy days, when the cow dug was not removed from the area around the camp, I didn't like walking about so much because I always stepped in something. That made me feel yucky.

Cattle camp life afforded many opportunities for traditional, informal education and cultural transmission. It was a speical place where boys and girls grew as responsible persons and social beings within Nilotic society.

The boys hunted animals such as squirrels, small gazelles, and rabbits. The girls gathered wild berries and dug for wild roots. The same *toich* (flood plain) offered grazing land for the livestock and yielded a rich variety of wild spinach-like greens for our mothers. There too, the traditional doctor dug for roots and harvested healing herbs. Some of the bitter roots were such strong medicine that only the sick children who already had strong stomachs and livers could digest them.

Older people told the children that evil things made their homes in the ground, the forest, and the river, but the *jok* (the evil spirit) gave us children little cause for concern. Nevertheless, following the advice of the adults, I did not go to the river or into the forest at night.

As the we children hunted, fished, and played games of hide and seek in the *toich*, we did not notice the impoverishment of the land caused by heavy rains washing away the topsoil. Still, I do not remember being hungry as a child, there was always more than enough to eat: *aoodo* milk shake, a piece of dry meat or fish, and a variety of fruit. We ate new corn cooked on the cob and boiled groundnut (peanuts). There was dry dura (sorghum) cooked with beans, stamped and broken into bits and cooked in the fresh butter, or crushed and ground to powder. We ate pumpkins, wild vegetables, squash, eggs, sour milk, fresh warm milk (straight from the cow), sesame butter mixed with sour milk, and a host of other delectable foods. Such variety! Such ready availability!

In 1993, when I returned to southern Sudan I found my people starving. I began to question. What happened to the life I knew? What happened to the rich life of my people? When I was growing up, I did not know of relief food—food from other parts of the world. The rich abundance I recalled from my childhood had been replaced by want and suffering all over the Nilotic land. Now I found my people without the laughter and peace they once had.

After that visit, the memory remained in my mind of the rich life of the past, but now there were no words to describe it. My days fell into nightmarish despair. I saw no days that would move on towards laughter, except in the stale memory of times of peace. I prayed that my people would return to the abundance of the past and see the importance of building peace. I was hurt by the twisted anguish of my crippled homeland. I wanted to clear my voice and sing a song of comfort to my homeland.

In the twenty years since that first visit, every time I return to southern Sudan and look at the women and children, I know they still are hurting. I see suffering in the silence of their eyes. Their condition has not changed over the long years of endless war. I still see no life, but the slow death of my dazed homeland, the southern Sudan.

The Nilotic people of southern Sudan claim the soil of their homeland with the blood of their young people, but their leaders are scattered around the world as refugees, searching for comfort. Being a refugee and also Black in America is a struggle. Many of our people who make their homes in new lands find rejection, because of the fear that we will take away jobs and economic benefits of the host country.

Many questions trouble me, but I hear no answers, only the voice of doom in my homeland from a liberation movement with a vision of terror. I see leadership that puts guns into the hands of children. Where are the newborn southern Sudanese leaders who can claim the hands of our children? Where are the leaders our children can trust? Where are the peacemakers, because they shall save lives? The peacemakers will bring back a smile to the faces of little ones and reclaim childhood, as I can, remembering my childhood evenings of singing and laughter.

In the evenings in the cattle camp, we sat around the fire or the *luak* (cattle barn). Each hut had a purpose, but we did not call them "dining room" or "bedroom." The big hut was the *luak*; men took care of it. Behind the *luak* was the family hut, where most of the activities of living took place. Women did the cooking and managed the family affairs here. In front of the family hut stood a small wall where three stones created a cooking surface. The three stones were arranged in a triangular shape, forming seat for the cooking pot.

In the mornings, there would be a slow burning fire of dried cow dung to heat the pot. Stamped *dura* (sorghum) would be cooking to make *kuan Naath* (sorghum meal), to be eaten with warm milk right from the cow. This was morning food.

In the afternoon, the women would start cooking a pot of beans and groundnut, the nutritious staple food of the Nilotic people. This was to be our supper, which ended with the drinking of milk.

When food was being served, the men all sat cross-legged on the floor in the *luak*. Women never sit cross-legged. They sit with their legs either folded back to one side or else straight out. People eat in groups, the men in one and the children and women in another. At supper time, the children would hardly be able to keep their eyelids from closing. The voice of the grandpa or grandma would bring in the once upon a times, becoming sewn in sleep until the next day, when the morning started again with the sound of early birds singing.

I plead for that morning when I wake up and see children playing and singing again in peace in southern Sudan. I look forward to embrace the day of my dreams, the day when the children of southern Sudan are safe and secure with their families. This is the day when they will know that this is their land, and the soil will bring back their livelihood.

When I was a child I recited and learned all the names of my ancestors. I am a Nilotic woman with five mothers in our family. But there are many, many more grandmothers, grandfathers, uncles, aunts, brothers, sisters, and cousins. With Nilotic people, I have been taught that I must always count everybody who is related to me in any way. The sum of all these people is a whole nation.

The River Nile

Nature's gift to the Nilotic people is the Nile. The Nile River system has greatly influenced the Nilotic way of life. Easy access to water and grasses for animals has made the land better suited for animal husbandry than for crop production, though the Nilotic people have a mixed economy. All the Nilotic children love water. Wading in the shallows and trying to catch small catfish was a favorite pastime of ours. Often I would be certain I had one in my hands but, when I opened them, I found them empty. These tiny fish were small, slippery, and swift, slicing through little fingers clumsily closing in a vain attempt to capture them.

Finding no fish in my hands was a puzzle, "Where did it go? I had it right in my hands." Children would bet as to who would be the first to make a catch or who would catch the biggest fish.

I often went to the Nile River with my sisters and friends to play. I still remember very clearly how we enjoyed the cool air by the river. I had a height advantage over my playmates, some of whom were just a little over five feet tall. I had reached 5' 11" by the time I was 12 years old. Now, I am 6' 1" tall. Playing in the river, the children fell naturally into groups, those who were tall enough to wade across and those who were too short to cross alone. Then there were those who were afraid, the cowards whose hearts pounded like drums at the very idea of crossing the river.

Going to the river alone was one activity our parents strongly discouraged. They said we might drown or slip in the mud and hurt ourselves. Or we might catch a cold from getting wet on cold mornings. Or we might be eaten by hippos and crocodiles. But worse than that, any child who went to the river at night might be called into the water by the "River Woman" whose dangerous beauty drew people into the depth of her magnetic eyes, and sucked them into the world deep under the river where she made her home. Beneath the water, her sons and daughters were waiting to be married to inhabitants of the outside world. This story was told so that the children should not go to the river alone at night without adult supervision. As children, we believed the story and had faith that our elders wanted what was best for us.

A river is a wonderful thing to have. I remember the beauty and the richness of the Nile, the tasteless, dirty-white foamy sweep of water gurgling, spiraling and spilling over the boulders to rest at one of the many elbows of the river, catching its breath and breaking into sweat, before moving away, making room for wearier water. I remember the yellowish-green color of frogs, and small black frogs, and bigger frogs with jerky, graceful movements. There were dark green weeds whose yellowish-white tender stalks, just above the roots, are such sweet delicacies. We swam in the river, bathed in the river, fetched water from it, and washed clothes in it. The cattle also waded in and drank from it. I do not know how the water in the river remains clean when so many villages make use of it in so many different ways. The Nilotic people took care of the river, because people never threw dirt in it. The land and the river were there for them.

The land provided a lifestyle and self-sufficiency and gave autonomy to the household. In many practical ways, the Nilotic people were bound to the land and to the family structures favoring cooperation. Despite the severe disadvantages that people faced on the land, people saw their rural lifestyle as safer than a new one based on urban wage-labor. Land, as I was taught to see it, was regarded as something reliable and controllable. Long term investments were made in cattle; short term investments were made on the land. In that way people were able to control their own lives.

Principles of Village Life

The most universal aspect of rural life in southern Sudan is the village. This pattern of social organization is found in all African societies. Max Gluckman and associates (1949) wrote:

Once social understanding occurs in a ethnic group, whatever their environment and the social structure is, this is the village—a discrete group of people who usually reside in adjacent huts, who recognize allegiance to their elders, and who have a corporate identity with other similar groups.

Members of the village community are normally linked together by social ties of kinship and affinity. The one Nuer word *maar* means kinsmen, relative, or personal kindred. *Maar* can indicate not only the blood relationhip, but also the relationship of close friendship. These ties define a community. Nilotic descent is patrilineal. In the early days, and even today, all members of a village community have to prove a genealogical relationship. All patrilineal kinship links figure strongly. One calls both one's father's and one's own brothers by the same family name. The Nilotics also consider one's father's brother's children as effectively equivalent to one's own siblings.

The largest patrilineally structured group among the Nilotic is a loose conglomeration of households consisting of the families of brothers and patrilineal first cousins, all known collectively by one name of their common grandfather. Residence, therefore, is patrilocal. This village community becomes the center of life, and members cooperate economically in many ways. Each family has its own fields, but cooperative labor among the members of a patrilineal extended family is common, as is also mutual aid, in the form of sharing both food and resources, such as money. Cattle are separately owned but are often herded together. The Nilotic village life is glued to any known kinship links between two individuals as the basis for mutual aid, support, and goodwill. Nilotic people maintain close ties with their families throughout their lives, even if they live in different communities.

Among the Nilotic, a person expects to be able to call upon anyone for whom he or she uses a kinship term for assistance in times of need or for help in endeavors that require collective labor. The combined principles of age and affinity make members who are age-mates prime candidates for cooperation and mutual aid. There is a tendency for members of same village to convert friendships to ties of affinity where it is convenient. Female kin also make conscious attempts to be married into villages where their sisters or other relatives have already married. This proximity enables female kin to be in a position to give and receive cooperation and mutual aid. A sister will often help with domestic duties her sick or pregnant sister living in a nearby village. Mutual-aid ties and friendly solidarity are particularly marked among the husbands of sisters. These patterns of cooperation mean that men or women who are of the same age often develop special relationships.

An individual can gain residence in any village through any one of three types of relationships: shared common experience; ties of friendship or acquaintance; and kinship, marriage, affinal ties, or clanship. Each family is linked to a clan. It is considered good among Nilotic people for a family to extend its patrilineal relationships by intermarrying with as many clans as possible. Intermarriage thus builds a network of clan alliances, with women as key players in keeping harmony and ethnic unity. My father, a Nuer, was able to reside in Dinka country after he married my mother. His in-laws became his strong kin.

An individual member retains his or her place in the group as long as he or she displays good character and appropriate behavior. The significance of such requirements becomes crucial when one realizes that a village community in southern Sudan is considered more than a mere social grouping. It is also an "ethical unit" whose goodness depends upon the character of its members. The implications of this concept of the village are far-reaching and of great importance, since the most cherished element in village living is what Callen Young (1937) calls the "great-hearted comradeship." This means that if the village members fear that an individual's conduct might "spoil" the group, then the community will not hesitate to withhold or withdraw rights of association.

The rules in the composition of Nilotic communities based on village kinship are now open to change. The changes are owing to the impact of Christianity and Islam, the rise of urban dwelling, and increased trade.

The rules of urban residence are drastically different from those of the rural residence. In the village community, one lives among a community of relatives, while in urban areas, qualifications for settling in a particular area are based mainly on economic factors. This has led to a situation where people in the urban setting are grouped into communities based upon economic stratum, social class, or religious affiliation. This new "kinship" is not based upon old ties of ethnicity or clan, but upon common interests of the new environment and new life.

These urban dwellers, who only yesterday were integral members of kin-based village communities, still belong to these communities at heart. While the urban groupings are developing into new forms of kin-based community groupings, people in urban areas essentially live as individuals and survive on what they or members of their nuclear family can provide. Some urban dwelling Nilotics have adapted the Western/Christian or the Islamic way of life. For example, the growing tendency among urban Nilotics is to have only one wife, rather than multiple wives.

Ultimately, when all else fails, the urban Nilotic may turn for help to their traditional institutions with rules and regulations of eligibility. This situation has caused some urban dwelling Nilotic people to live in two worlds. They are physically living in towns, but their lives are governed by traditional village customs.

I know well the tension of living in two worlds. All my life I have gone to church on Sunday mornings. I also have participated in traditional African rituals and ceremonies. My whole experience has been one of adapting to and incorporating the modern with the traditional to create a new way of life. Many African villages now are facing these challenges, since some of their relatives live in villages and others live in the urban areas. The residents increasingly make functional compromises between Western urbanism and traditional African patterns of social organization. Nevertheless, towns are still foreign to the majority of Nilotic people.

In all these efforts to merge town and rural life into one social system, the individual participants have relied upon kinship as the basic institution within which to develop the new social network. Traditional kinship institutions perform two basic functions for the

Nilotic urban dweller. First, they provide means through which one may gain help from others in times of need or misfortune and second, they provide the only identifiable means for preserving one's family, kinship, and ethnic identity. Traditional kinship institutions are "survival kits" in a strange and sometimes cruel urban world. Through them, the individual is able to develop multifunctional personal links with other individuals who are mutually bound by the same institutions of family, kinship, and ethnicity.

In addition to Christianity, Islam, and urban influence, trade has been an important avenue bringing change to Nilotic villages. Trade relationships traditionally existed between the Nilotic people and their neighbors to the south and north, the Bantu people and the Arab Massirya. Certain points along the boundaries were recognized as trading centers, as were points within Nilotic land among the Nuer, Dinka, Shilluk and Anuak. The trade primarily involved foodstuffs. In times of food shortage, men would travel into the territory of neighboring ethnic groups to exchange small livestock for surplus grain. During the first half of the nineteenth century, the Nilotic also traded for metal implements, hoes, axes, and weapons. The Arab Massirya and Nilotic people also traded for beads.

Other items in demand were cattle, pots, dried fish, hides, tobacco, and crafted items. Nilotic women traditionally made clay pots. Men traditionally worked in wood, making such things as three-legged stools and knobbed clubs. Few baskets are made in Nilotic land, most of them made by women. Both men and women do leather work. Men make cowhide ropes and women make leather clothing. Manufactured furniture, such as beds, tables, and chairs, are now commonly found in Nilotic households. Western-style clothing is worn by both sexes, except the very old, who still wear the traditional *lawa,* an outfit consisting of two printed, cotton rectangular cloths, one wraped around the shoulders and the other wrapped around the waist.

The village community is the center of Nilotic life. In southern Sudan, as in many other African countries, even a casual look at the principles of this way of life reveals that people know how to deal with their daily problems. As I closely observe my people today, its is clear to me that the community-based pattern based on cooperation produces relevant and effective services for the people. I want to stress, however, that the society of the Nilotic people of southern Sudan is in transition. Both rural and urban patterns of social organization are changing and adapting to a new, wider social field. Professor Vincent Ostrom has emphasized that, "Africa must rediscover it indigenous patterns: Things people know and were relevant to them, and allow them to go on with their normal lives."

Community-wide Roles

The community-wide roles of the Nilotic people fall within the following categories: ritual leaders, diviners, and practitioners of traditional medicine, judicial leaders, and political leaders. Priests or custodians, ceremonial elders or ritual experts may be either male and female. The male is responsible for performing and overseeing all details of men's ceremonies and ceremonies involving both genders. He does not have authority over women's ceremonies.

These are organized and overseen by female ritual experts.

Traditional weddings must involve both a male and female ritual expert, although the male is considered to be in charge. The position of the female ritual expert is less formal than is that of the priest; nonetheless, because of their social knowledge and reputation among women, female ritual experts can attain significant influence in a local community.

Traditional medicine is an art practiced by both men and women. The Nilotic traditional doctor, or herbalist, employs both rituals and remedies concocted from local plants to treat conditions such as colds, fever, diarrhea, nausea, headache, backache, menstrual cramps, and infertility. Nowadays Western-trained medical practitioners, the majority of them men, are consulted for illnesses that used to be treated by herbalists.

Community meetings are conducted by the village elders. Traditionally, women attended in the role of observers, usually sitting in a cluster in a corner of the gathering. Women spoke publicly only when they were direct participants in litigation or were called as a witness. When they did speak, they generally used the opportunity to guide men who might otherwise manipulate the situation. Despite traditional limitations, Nilotic women have held a certain amount of prestige, influence, and even power within the community.

Today, the pattern of women's roles in the wider community is changing. Among some ethnic groups in southern Sudan, the women have lower status than men. Among other ethnic groups women are given equal status. Among still other groups they serve as leaders in their communities. Ironically, while women are participating more in the political arena at the local level, they are losing some of the institutions through which they once had power to affect community life. Furthermore, the role of ritual expert, which gave some women recognition as leaders in the community, is on the decline. Western education has opened opportunities for women to participate in Western-derived political institutions and as members of governing boards of schools, health clinics, community water supply, and other institutions.

The Nilotic women retain their female identity on the basis of family relationships. Women therefore gain more than do men from maintaining boundaries between the Nilotic and the neighboring ethnic groups. This is one reason why women are the keepers of traditional values of Nilotic society. Among the Nilotic, married women have an expectation of partnership with their husbands in matters of home life. Keeping an extended family group together requires constant attention, negotiation, and compromise on the part of women. Through their solildarity, Nilotic women can win the respect of everyone in the community. This is especially true in times of conflict when women use their kinship links to keep their communities together.

The majority of Western scholars judge the traditional lives of African people by modern Western values. By that standard, Africans indeed have hard lives. Yet this can be distorting. Most of the literature written about African people, especially women, is written by non-African scholars with little or no understanding of women's lives. The impression given in this literature is that village women are drudges, mindlessly doing their daily work with nothing to talk about or look forward to. As a Nilotic woman, I know that this is not the case.

The modern African woman would rebel against carrying loads of firewood home while her husband sat inside the house entertaining his friends. Yet the women of my mother's generation kept the traditions; they worked long hours and they never complained. In summer they walked long distances to bring water from far away water holes. The men, in turn, spent countless hot days and nights, looking after the cattle, hunting to kill and bring home food, defending their families from prowling enemies, and hiking long distances to bring home needed supplies.

In the Nilotic culture, the work of the women is generally respected and honored, for the men know very well that they could not live without it. The Nilotic people consider it a great honor that the women should bear and rear children, ensuring that there will be generations to come. In the social life of the Nilotic people, a household is judged not only by the bravery and generosity of the man, but also by the kindness and work habits of the woman. Even the wife of a man with fewer cattle could find honor among her people by being a good mother and a trusted member of her community. These values traditionally are passed from mother to daughter through daily experience, but wih the changes facing the Nilotic people, writing down our traditions will help the next generation.

Village Leadership

Nilotic communities are organized around a group of elder kinsmen. A few individual village elders hold power in trust. As such, they not only perform administrative functions, but they also are symbols of the group's unity and solidarity. Elders have social knowledge and common sense knowledge about daily life accumulated through years of life experience. This indigenous knowledge is a pipeline to discovery, meaning, and appropriate action for the community.

The choice of an elder-leader is based upon some criteria. He must be a representative senior of the group, but if the oldest man lacks the necessary qualities, a younger one will be chosen. The elder-leader must be a hard worker, intelligent, wise, knowledgeable of clan traditions, and recognized for his leadership ability. The leader is the judge of his people; he mediates conflict and assures the well-being of the people. He must be fair and not discriminate according to lineage descent. The leader must understand that the community is made up of families, and the families of individuals, each representing a balance of complementary and interacting parts. He must get along with the members of his community and be a strong advocate for them. He must be a good public speaker, for he plays a leading role in major events such as marriage, death, and disputes over cattle, land, or water.

Being a leader among the Nilotic people is not a position of power for which men compete. In fact, if two should be equally qualified, each will stand back in deference to the other so as not to appear self-interested. In that case, one leader will be chosen by a consensus of the community members. Otherwise, the choice of an elder-leader is based on the perceptions and common knowledge of the possible leader's character and the respect in which he is held by the community.

Kinship Network

To understand the Nilotic pattern of social organization, one must see it in terms of kinship. Kinship is a communal bond that binds past, present, and future generations together. It is a web of relationships within which individual members stand in particular social relations to each other, and it is this bond which is the main governing social force. Callen Young (1937) wrote:

> The communal bond operates to prevent any self-separating individualistic development. The individual is in some way something more than a human unit; one is inseparable from those who were there before and equally inseparable from those who are to come after.

The institutions of kinship of Nilotic people could be seen as a comprehensive social insurance scheme in which the individual member finds not only broad-based companionship, but also social arrangements with mutual aid and reciprocal obligations. The whole system is supported by a complex set of relationships that are carefully woven into logical systems that have meaning for, and are understood by, all members. Each individual member of the kinship group is taught through social education to find one's rightful place. Every person is secure, since tradition demands that an individual appeals to his seniors or elders in times of trouble. By the rules of kinship, both paternal and maternal kinsmen are obligated to respond.

This tenet requires that individuals in a particular family group or village live not only with, but also for each other. In this way, their lives are meaningfully intertwined. It is this principle that is invoked in demanding participation in intra- and inter-group village cooperative activities such as work, parties, ceremonies, and celebrations. Learning to help and respect one another is the secret of togetherness.

When I think of all the pain that has been brought upon my people by the civil war, my heart weeps like a river. This cycle of destruction cannot go on. People can be made ignorant, but they cannot be kept ignorant. The people of southern Sudan know their rights. They know that democracy means living with freedom, respect for human rights, dignity, and common decency.

I wait for the day when the Sudanese civil war will be remembered as history.

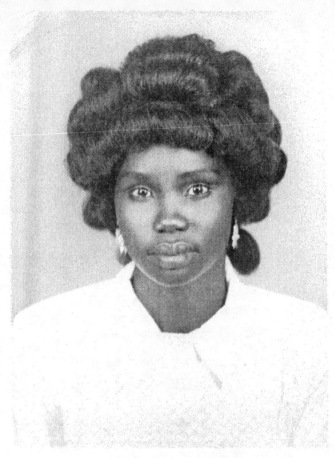

Julia Aker Benjamin Bil
after finishing teacher's training at Wed
Medani, 1972.

Chapter III

Going Away to School

I was afraid to leave my family, but I also wanted to go to school. Going to school changed my whole life.

My Early Learning

There is a Nuer proverb that says ability is wealth; knowledge is power. I am grateful that I can put down on paper what I remember from conversations of my parents' and other elders who helped shape my personality. Formal schooling taught me the "magic of the white people," as my uncle used to call it. When I first got a pen and paper, I quickly mastered the meaning of the symbols. My reading and writing improved until I was able to join the club of learned people. I became one of those magicians who have learned the magic of the white people.

Now as an adult, mother, and educator living in a new culture, why do I write? There are many reasons. First, I write to share my rich heritage with my children, and to inform others. Second, I write to keep the memories alive. Third, I write to honor my parents and my ancestors. And finally, I write to keep Africa and the Nilotic culture alive. In this book, I have drawn a picture of a vanished age, the character of Nilotic society, the foundations of their political system, the roots of the Sudanese civil war, how the scale of values has changed, and the outlook for young people.

I feel that my life is a journey, yet I have grown so accustomed to change and to the adjustments of relocation that it is often difficult to realize how rapidly the rivers of life have changed around me. I have struggled through these changes, raised a family in the midst of them, and have learned much through the experience. I have deep thoughts and feelings about it.

From earliest childhood, I was made to understand my environment and to follow in the footsteps of my mother. I was taught to know right from wrong, the first two words learned by the Nilotic children. In the Nilotic culture, mothers are close to their daughters, even to this day. It is also common for an aunt to take one of her nieces, or for a grandmother to take one of her grandchildren to raise. The traditional closeness enjoyed between the elders and their grandchildren gives the young generation exposure to the same values their parents were raised by. It also affords children a lot of love and attention. If the mother and father of a crying child were busy, there was usually a grandparent nearby who would find out what was wrong. This helps to explain how parents could handle half a dozen or more children crowded inside their huts on long rainy or dry season days and nights. The elders told stories, played games, and helped to occupy the minds of the children.

Tradition ruled, yet my father had different plans for his children. It was his dream that his children would receive a Western education. The majority of the people in our town had no idea of the usefulness of Western education; this was something they realized very late.

I admired my mother, but there was something missing. She could not read and write like my father.

But when I looked at my mother, I knew that she had all the knowledge and skills she needed to fulfill her roles. My mother's illiteracy caused me to question the value of the education she had received. This thought was further challenged by the fact that all of the English women were able to read and write. I felt that if my mother had been given a chance, she could have learned to read and write, but there were no schools for girls during my mother's youth.

I was almost seven years old when I was given my chance and trusted with the grown-up challenge of traveling to and attending school three hundred miles away from home. My first experience at school was frightening. The adults that took care of us were Roman Catholic nuns and a few female Sudanese workers—no father, no mother, no aunt, no grandparents. Then there were the school rituals, regulations, dormitories, schedule of classes, playtime, and after-school activities. I learned to answer to Julia, my Christian name, a name unrelated to my family history. The school was like a little village and the school children like herds of cattle.

I admired the nuns and missionaries' wives because of their education, but I really fell in love with learning.

Challenged by New Opportunities

One hot, humid, dusty afternoon when I was about 6 years old, I was sitting under a *raak* tree (a tree that bears edible fruits) playing games with my sister and our friends. We saw a Land Rover drive up and stop in front of my father's shop. There were three people in the vehicle, a black priest, a white priest, and a white nun. They all were dressed in long white clothing. I had grown up accustomed to seeing European women from Protestant churches wearing Western clothing, but this was the first time I had seen a European woman draped from head to toe. It shocked me right down to my toes, for to be visited by a nun and two priests was a great surprise. We knew why they had come, even though my father had never talked to any of us girls about attending school. My father already had four sons in school and all were doing very well, but my older sister Apanda (Martha) had closed the door for the females in our family. Apanda had gone to school for four years, but then quit to return to the cattle camp and live as a traditional Nilotic woman. That experience justified the idea that the best place for girls to learn was near their mothers, so that they could acquire the necessary family skills.

My interest in learning to milk a cow ended that day when I saw the white nun from Comboni Mission in front of our house. Sister Patricia was her name. She was on a hunt, trying to find families who might be interested in girls' education. She praised the Lord that day, because my father was willing to give her three of his daughters. My father called us in to meet Sister Patricia, the woman that would take the place of our mothers and train us into adulthood. I felt happy but at the same time did not want to show my mother how eager I was to go to school. Sister Patricia arranged to pick us up in a week, because she wanted to visit other villages and find other girls for the school.

Attending Nazareth Girls Elementary School in Wau, Bahr El Ghazal province broke the bond between my two sisters and I and the world we knew: our home and village. The school was too far away from home for us to return often. Catholic nuns, who spoke the

Dinka language with us during the first two years, ran the school. That eased the adjustment and maintained the harmony between the language of my home community and that of my formal education.

Girls' education was a new thing in the Dinka communities. Girls were generally not allowed to go to school, especially not far away from home. Girls are highly valued because they secure the bridewealth for the family. Our being in school around the nuns was a grave concern to many of our relatives and community members. My uncle Gum Machot was very angry when he learned that we had been sent to a mission school. He told my father that he had destroyed the family and that my brothers would not be able to marry because they had been deprived of their sisters' bridewealth. Often families rely on the bridewealth of their daughters to pay the bridewealth for their sons. Bridewealth means much to the Nilotic people. It is the primary means of distributing wealth. The cattle are passed from one family to another and from one community to another. This creates a large network and linkage among the communities.

In my third year of schooling, I was taught to speak English only. I was told not to speak my language. One of the most humiliating experiences a student could suffer was to be caught speaking Dinka in the vicinity of the school. The culprit was given corporal punishment: five to ten lashes with cane on bare buttocks for a boy and the same amount of lashes on the legs for a girl. It was either that or we were made to labor in the nun's or teacher's homes as servants for a week or two. The Nilotic people hate the idea of as servants.

How did the teachers catch the students? One student was given a stick, which she was to hand over to the one caught speaking her mother tongue. Whoever had the stick at the end of the day would sing the name of the one who had given it to her. The ensuing process brought out hunters and in the process, we taught to be traitors to our own immediate community. Something Nilotic people never do is spy on their own people. My language, home, and community became a disgrace according to the rules of my New World. I had to be "civilized." I learned to do things for myself, not for "us." I had to have more material wealth and was taught to give away only what I did not need. My well being became more important than "our" well being. To survive, everyone worked for himself or herself. This was the exact opposite of how I had been taught at home.

At school, achievement in spoken or written English was rewarded—prizes, prestige, applause—all tickets to higher realms. English became the measure of intelligence and ability in the arts, sciences, and other branches of learning. English became the main determinant of a child's progress up the ladder of formal education and into modern life.

Reading further exposed me to new ways. My first books were a series of four reading books: *The First African Oxford Reader*. I still remember the stories "An African School Girl" and "John Is a Good Cook." I was surprised to read about men cooking. My father never cooked anything in our house, and my mother never complained that it was his turn to cook. We also studied writing, arithmetic, home economics, fine arts, European music, history, and the geography of the European nations.

We recited dates of European wars, key events, names of dead and living queens and kings, cities, rivers, and physical features. We recited multiplication tables. Those who failed received lashes on their buttocks. Spelling was another killer subject. If a student missed five words, she received a great number of lashes. Our ebony skin hid every welt and bruise. The number of lashes a student managed to avoid depended on how fast a student advanced. The fast readers got away with few lashes, but the slow learners broke down in the middle of their reading with their tears streaming down their faces. They knew what was coming: either ten or more cane lashes on the buttocks or the flat side of a ruler brought down on the fingertips. The pain from that hit made some students scream at the top of their lungs.

There were no more hare and lion stories. No more evenings around the fire. In the minds of my European teachers, the image of the African was that of a child-like monster, incongruously violent, noisy, dishonest, inconsistent, and incapable of understanding the rule of law. This spirit must be tamed. These beliefs, no doubt, provided the justification for colonial rule as well as gave purpose to their educational system. From my point of view, it did not appear that the nuns particularly cared about educating the African girls; they just wanted them to learn to labor. We had to wash nuns' clothes and dishes, scrub floors, and work in the fields to produce our own food. Classroom learning was only a part of our school day, but those few hours of reading and writing had a very big influence on us.

On top of its base of racial discrimination, the colonial education system rose in a pyramid structure. There was a broad primary base, a narrowing secondary middle, and an even narrower university apex. This system created social classes, something not known to many African communities, especially in the

Nilotic communities. The more we learned, further we moved away from our community. We becoming *turuk* (modern and civilized) people and learning that our own culture was undesirable, primitive, and backward.

In school, I learned to be competitive. The nuns rewarded bright students. I was even made to skip a grade—I went from grade one to grade three. In this regard I followed the footsteps of my role models, my older brothers Barnaba Marial and George Maker. I was eager to go back home and share with my playmates the new things I was learning as my brothers did in school. My joy was therefore doubled on my first summer vacation in Akot, after spending nine months in school.

I admired my brothers tremendously. They were heroes to me and to all of the members of my family. I read all of the books they read. One summer they came home from school with Boy Scout uniforms. They taught us some of the things they learned: tying a knot, Morse Code, and marching. They were perfectionists and we, the young sisters and brothers, proudly looked up to them as they led their small troop of followers. Among our village playmates, my brothers were the undisputed leaders. They were bright and athletic. As their sister, I was under their protection, and also at their service.

From very early in life, I was made aware that my life would be much changed for the better if I did my schoolwork well. I could go on to higher education; I could be somebody. At a tremendous personal sacrifice, my parents gave their children an opportunity that they themselves never had.

On the last day of my fourth year of elementary school I stayed in my classroom the whole afternoon. When I did not return to my dormitory, my sister

Margaret Aliu came looking for me. When the bell rang at three o'clock, all students went to where the whole school assembled. In that December 1963 gathering, our class of thirty-eight girls waited to hear their fate. Our hearts beat like drums, because on this day we would find out who was eligible to come back next year and who would stay home for good. There were no second chances given to those who did not pass the first time. We students hated this time of the year, with its finality of humiliation and exaltation. Our teacher Sister Angela read the list. She read first the names of those who had passed:

"Julia Aker Benjamin Bil,
Margaret Aliu Benjamin Bil,
Mary Atido Alfred Barjuok,
Christiania Nadi John Gala,
Inge Angong Magorbok."

We had passed our fourth year of schooling. We were now learned young ladies. I was thrilled! I ran out of the hall across the schoolyard, not waiting for the assembly to finish. My feet were flying high as I ran to my room to savor the great new day of my life's achievement.

On the following day we traveled back to our hometown. When we arrived home, the first thing we shared with our parents was the good news. We had passed the national examination and we would enter the intermediate school next year. A month later my father received a letter from the Ministry of Education, Southern Regional Office in Juba. I had been awarded a certificate of achievement for being at the top of my class.

Since that time, my learning has advanced to where I am today. My family gave that opportunity to me, and it opened other doors to further opportunities that I eagerly accepted to participate fully in my new life.

In the intermediate level, school discipline remained a high priority for the nuns. Sister Pauline, known as Mother Pauline, was the headmistress of the school. She was in her mid forties and especially strict. When the students saw her coming, her long white gown flapping as she walked, we knew someone was in big trouble.

Mother Pauline was a quick learner. In two years she learned several Sudanese languages. She spoke Dinka, Ndogo, Belanda, Kresh, Bongo and others. Some students admired her because of her courage and ability to learn the culture and to know the people of Sudan. As she began learning Dinka words, Mother Pauline began calling the students names. One day she said *apeth diit*, big witches, and *abeel diit,* big fool. The students did not take her name-calling seriously because she couldn't pronounce these words well and didn't seem to understand what they meant. Whenever she said *apeth diit*, a crowd of girls would break out with laughter. Mother Pauline thought she was being funny and that the girls liked it. She enjoyed repeating her new Dinka words over and over. She sounded so funny and stupid.

At the evening church service, those who wanted to confess their sins went the confession altar. Among them was Mother Pauline, who had been cursing the whole day. We girls laughed, knowing she had used the word *apeth* (witches) many, many times that day. Now she had to go to the priest to confess her sin. She must have praised her Lord for being so kind as to forgive her.

After Mother Pauline learned how to speak Dinka very well, she did not use the word *apeth* regularly, but found others such as *ran raac* bad person or *jok raac* devil with which to scold us.

My whole fifth year of school was spent agonizing over rulers and canes. Everybody was eager to get to the end of the year. Relief came with vacation in mid December, marking the end of the school year. At this time the students said goodbye to each other and to the nuns. This was a hard time for students, especially among those who had formed close friendships. If one had failed it was heartbreaking, because she knew she would not see her friends again the following year.

In early April, school started again. There were new nuns as well as the old nuns who had not gone back home to Italy. Those who were strong enough to survive the malaria fever somehow stayed well and strong enough to perform their duties.

One of the things I worked very hard to avoid was the lash. I pushed myself to complete all of my work. I trained my mind to be tough, so I could recite spelling words quickly and correctly. I learned that hard work paid off, leaving me with only minor mistakes and few lashes.

What I really did not understand was how the nuns could be so cruel to us. These big, strong women pulled their strength together, hitting us small children seemingly without any feeling in their hearts. This was a mystery to other students as well. My mother hit me, but never so hard that the bruises had to be nursed. We students never questioned the school discipline. We took it as from our parents.

91

Despite the strong discipline, I grew fond of school. My sisters and I looked forward to returning at the end of each summer holiday and meeting our friends. We also enjoyed going back to school because we got new clothes, shoes, and many other things that the other children admired. For our return my mother packed soaps and food. She prepared dried *kisra*, a food like cornflakes made out of sorghum flour. She prepared peanut and sesame butter in tins, a few bags of sugar, bags of dates, roasted peanuts, and honey for our snacks. For us girls it was an adventure, but my parents understood what Western education would mean for the future of Sudan.

A major change came in 1964. When Sudan became an independent country (1956), all schools run by Christian missionaries were taken over by the national government and placed under the Ministry of Education. This was the situation when I first went to the Comboni Mission School with Mother Pauline. By 1964, however, missionaries' relations with the Islamic-dominated government had deteriorated across the board. The government accused the missionaries of fueling the ongoing southern rebellion.

Under the Ministry of Interior's orders on February 27, 1964, Christian missionaries were expelled from southern Sudan. Our school suddenly lost all of its teachers and was placed under police guard for an entire month. Later teachers from the North came in to start the school again. The government provided this education free to all children. This is when southern Sudanese Arabic education started.

Our Arab masters came south, bringing radical change. Overnight, all of Sudan became an Islamic nation. Arabic replaced English (the colonial language) as the language of instruction in school. I had no choice but to accept the change and adapt to the new authority, which made it all the more evident that the language of formal education was not the language of my people. Actually, Arabic is more than a language. It is Islamic culture. Everyone bowed before it in deference.

I was told again and again that the European language and civilization I had learned from the nuns was imperialistic and very, very bad. These teachers also carried whips in their hands, and I was made to understand what Arabic language and the Arabic culture meant. It was a nightmare, but I struggled to adjust to these new ways.

There were also big changes in the school administration. The government brought workers to clean and provide services for students. These were tasks, that under the administration of the Comboni sisters, students had done for themselves. Cleaning the rooms, cooking the food, and drawing water from the wells were now done by government workers. The schoolchildren adored this aspect of the new system, but their parents worried that the children would become lazy. In our school, a number of girls did not return the following year because their parents would not let them.

When I was young, I heard many stories about the Arab slave traders and their cruel ways of treating Africans. The majority of Nilotic children grew up afraid of Arabs, imagining that they were a kind of ogre-race that killed and enslaved people. Images of cruel Arabs tormenting the Nilotic people were woven into the folk tales and into the swamp of fear hiding in the back of the children's' minds. Fear cried out to the children from its hiding place, "Never trust an Arab." This was a consistent theme.

It was only through learning the Arabic language that I was able to control my fear of Arabs. The door of my mind swung open, and through the shapes and figures of language I began to see, to know, and to confront the vague figures of fear hidden in my mind.

I spent days and nights learning the Arabic characters and writing from right to left. We were given old books to read that had been donated by Arab countries. I read books about great Arab astrologers, demonologists, alchemists, magicians, and atheists. I learned about Mohammed, the founder of Islam, the Caliphates, and the new religious system. Islam means submission, and I came to understand my new masters. The content of these books never allowed me to have peace. They taught me nothing about my people or about the modern world.

These books seemed to turn into the flesh of Arab monsters, but I no longer faced them as a little girl. I was becoming a woman. With my growing understanding of the Arab/Islamic civilization came a growing desire to stand up for my own rights and to reclaim my own identity. I wanted to be who I am—an African, proud of my own civilization. This was how I faced my future—learning to read and write in Arabic.

After I finished my intermediate studies at the school in Wau, I entered my first year of college at Wed Medani. It was my first time to attend a school in northern Sudan. It was not a nice experience. Southern students were a minority, so we were given segregated accommodations in one hall of the dormitory. Our hall was under the supervision of the principal, Amina

Jaafer Bakit. She was middle-aged, unmarried, and living in the dormitory with students.

The majority of northern teachers believed that the people of the South were still as backward and wild as animals. They believed we had no culture and no rules for living. Some of them said, "these Africans from the tropical jungle have no laws and must be taught to behave like people."

At Wed Medani, we Southerners were never allowed to speak our own languages. If Amina heard any student using language other than Arabic, that student was sentenced to labor for seven days. The guilty one had to cut the grass in the schoolyard or arrange sidewalk bricks in the hot Sahara sun. Amina was ignorant about the South and its culture. She believed that there were no towns in the South, that the people lived in villages in the jungle, and that they did not take baths. If ever there was something bad smelling in the dormitory, she thought it was those Southern students. She would order all of us to come out of our rooms to take a bath, while she stood in the hallway to make certain everyone obeyed. I wanted to remind her that the River Nile she depended upon for water had its origin in the South, and that at any given moment there were countless Africans in it taking baths.

Akot Village and Social Change

Before the Arabs changed everything in 1964, there was a boys' school run by the Episcopal missionaries in Akot our hometown. While this little school had contributed to social change in the area, Akot was full of boys who had either not gone to school at all or who had dropped out. These boys formed a group who made fun of the schoolboys and called them names. They called schoolboys either *amil or ashkal,* Arabic words for workers, or else *kadim,* a servant. The unschooled boys considered themselves above the schoolboys and discouraged them from attending school. They considered that those who attended school would work for others all of their lives. My father had a different understanding about school and made it clear that schooling was a priority for his children. Now when I look back, I think this was a blessing.

The unschooled boys also called schoolgirls bad names, but my sisters and I felt safe in the shadow of our brothers' protection. Nobody dared to mess around with the sisters of our brothers. We were the only girls who were respected by the village boys.

My father was the first of his family to set foot inside a classroom building. He often told us stories of his youth and of the benefits of Western education. His success in trading had been the subject of some jealousy among the local northern Sudanese traders. He was the first African in our town to own a business and to dress his wives in European clothes: skirts, blouses, and high-heeled shoes. He was the first to keep his cattle in town, when other Dinka kept their cattle on the *toich* (flood plain).

In our town the Episcopal Church also organized adult literacy classes. The purpose was to teach women to read the Bible. One day my mother sent me to tell one of the missionaries, Miss Jean, that the women would like her to come to our house for the next meeting. Miss Jean was in charge of the women's ministry. I did not want to go to Miss Jean and give her the message orally. I found the verbal carrying messages particularly demeaning. I would rather have died than to be seen as an illiterate person. I felt that our family dignity was at stake, our intelligence in question, and our very sense of worth challenged. This was embarrassing to me. I would never have allowed my mother to deliver a message orally. I knew everyone in our little town and the opinion they held of my family mattered greatly to me.

It mattered that I came from a family with an educated father. I knew why everyone looked up to him. It was not because of his wealth, but because of his education and involvement in community affairs. My father demonstrated concretely that schooling was not a bad thing. On the contrary, education was a profitable venture. The head Chief Malek Malual always came to our house to have tea with my father and discuss community affairs. I wanted my family to act appropriately, but it was not possible to explain this to my mother. I was afraid to disobey her. As soon as I was out of my mother's sight, I went to my father and got a piece of paper and a pen to write the note. I wrote and carried the note to Miss Jean with competence. I acted as a self-respecting person.

The next time I was sent to take the message to Miss Jean I did the same thing, wrote a note. This time my mother was sick and could not go to class. I was on the way to Miss Jean's with the note, and not very far from our home, when I met some friends. We started talking, running, and laughing. I grasped the note tightly in my left hand, but before I realized it, the note had disappeared. My heart started pumping.

"*Warga*, the note," I yelled.

"*Warga ee ngu*, what note?" asked one of the girls.

Now I was in trouble. I told the girls my mother had sent me with a note to Miss Jean telling her that she was not going to class because she was sick. Now the note was gone.

I did not go to Miss Jean.

The women all went to class, but my mother was not there. Miss Jean asked the women if anyone had passed by my mother's place, but nobody had. They were concerned, so when the class was over they all went to check on my mother. That's when my mother learned that I had not taken the message to Miss Jean as I was told.

I had no solution to my dilemma. I kept staring at my hand as if that would make the note come back. My pride would not allow me to go and speak the message to Miss Jean. With a couple of my friends, I retraced my steps, searching for the note. It was a hopeless task, since that day the winds were blowing hard and a small piece of paper was not likely to be sitting on the ground waiting for us. We tried every test. We spit saliva on one hand, and started counting, *tok, ku row, ku diak* (one, two, three), *taak teen, ku taak teen, yen akin* (I go this way, go that way, and here it is). We tried spitting in our palm and hitting the saliva with two of the fingers of the other hand, thus making it fly onto the ground. This would indicate the direction in which the lost object might be found. We followed the direction, still hoping to find the note. We had no luck at all.

An hour had passed since my departure from home, so I made the desperate decision to disappear from my mother for a while. Actually, I stayed hidden for a very long time, scared as a little kitten. There was no doubt that I was a candidate for a whipping that day. How would I explain my not delivering the message at the right time? Oh, how clearly I saw the way to save myself. My little heart told me, "Disappear, disappear."

As it was growing darker, I was at loose ends. I had no idea where to go. I knew that no one would welcome me to their home without first asking questions, telling my parents, or dragging me back home. In fact, I was well aware that any adult who saw me at this late hour would take me home. These were disadvantages to living in a small community, where everybody knew your name, knew everyone else's children, and knew everybody's business. People never kept their mouths shut about other people's business, especially when that business concerned a child. I felt the limitations imposed on me by my environment.

My friends had left me long ago, going about their legitimate business, mindful of their own positions with their families. So there I was, hiding from people and afraid of hyenas as well. I realized there was a vast difference between the darkness elsewhere and the darkness in the vicinity of my home. In a Nilotic village, there are no homeless people. I was so scared because I wanted to become one. I thought I could leave home, but remain within my home area. That way, if I was in danger, I could scream and get help from my family.

I found myself heading in the direction of my home. It was quite dark by the time I rounded some of my friends' houses. Then I came within sight of the dark shape of the two-room building that belonged to my mother. I peeked in to see who was there. The person I saw was my sister, Nyanlath. She had a big mouth and would tell everybody where I was. I jumped back and almost fell into the garbage hole in back of the house. At that moment a pack of dogs hunting for leftover food came running toward me. Weak with fear, I found myself yelling, "*jok, jok, jok*, dog, dog, dog!" I faked being chased by dogs.

Coming home was a relief, but I still faced the problem that would come in the morning. Should I tell my mother what had happened? She probably already knew everything, and I would have to face the consequences of my actions regardless. Whatever punishment was coming, I resolved to take it.

"Nyakal, where have you been?" asked my mother, using my nickname Malakal Girl. (Malakal is my father's hometown.) My father loved this name because it reminded him of his origin. "I told you many times to tell the truth, no matter what happens," my mother scolded. I was speechless. I did not want to add more to what I already had done by telling stories. I was given a small punishment. My mother told me to fetch water for ten days. This meant I had to fill up all the drinking pots every morning and evening. I thanked her for being so considerate, because I hated being whipped. And I learned my lesson.

As a child, I was always eager to become *akim* (a nurse or a doctor). My dreams of helping people through community services were influenced by the wives of the missionaries, who were known for helping and caring for the sick. When either my brother or sister was sick, I would act as a nurse, preparing the bed, bringing water, and doing whatever it took to make that person feel better.

One summer holiday, when I came back from boarding school, my uncle came to visit us. He became sick with malaria. I was in fourth grade, and I could read and write very well. I also had some medical knowledge and knew what to do when somebody was sick with an upset stomach or a high fever. I told my uncle, "I know what to do to make you better. Right now, don't eat solid food, don't drink any milk, but drink fresh lemon juice with sugar and a little salt." It was a joke to my uncle—a little girl playing and trying to be nice to her uncle.

My uncle, who did not believe very much in modern medicine, did not see malaria as a killer, but as something he could shake off with hard work and drinking bitter roots. When my father came back from the shop, he asked my uncle to go to the clinic to get some anti-malaria medicine. I told my father that Uncle did not need to go to the clinic because I had already given him the treatment. I handed my father the prescription I had written. It read:

Uncle Gum Machot:
High fever and upset stomach,
no solid food but drink a lot of liquid
with sugar and salt.

My father read the paper and was impressed, but he told me that the only way my uncle was going to get better was to go to the clinic to get anti-malaria medicine. Then he said: "Come, let's take your uncle to the clinic." My uncle was very surprised that my father understood what I had written. He always thought that reading was the magic of white people.

My father told the story to the medical assistant at the clinic, who also read the paper and was very impressed with what I had written. He told my father, "This is the person who will take my place when I am old." He did not change the written treatment, but added a treatment of anti-malaria medicine. From that day, my uncle changed his attitude about girls schooling. Whenever he visited us, he would hold my head with his two hands, blow air and sprinkle water on my head, hands, and feet, which is a Nilotic way of blessing. He prayed that I would do well in school and become *akim* (a doctor) to save the old people from malaria.

Taking my Place in Building the Future

Before Western education could become widely accepted, the Nilotic people had to overcome a number of obstacles. Western education was seen as a threat to the Nilotic people's way of life, not only because it undermined customary values, but also because it took young men and women out of the fields and cattle camps and put them into the classrooms to become scholars. However, some parents, like my father, encouraged their children to go to school. These parents realized that their world was changing and that the future held different challenges for their children than it had held for them. They understood that without schooling, their children would be able to get jobs in the modern nation of Sudan. I think they saw that only way we could survive as a people was to learn how to live with others.

Western education clearly offered a different way of looking at life. As far as a Nilotic is concerned, there are two selves, the collective self and the private self. When a malaise affects an individual, the whole group is substantially affected. If an individual succeeds, everyone has succeeded. One's experiences are felt and shared by everyone. I was able to dedicate my collective self to my traditions and learning how to live with other people, and my private self to my education and learning modern ways.

An individual in the Nilotic culture, whether in the private or the collective sense however, does not have the final say about his or her own life. The activities one undertakes are conducted in the context of the whole group. The individual must be aware of what the group expects, and act accordingly. Although the society acknowledges each person as a unique individual with unique qualities, talents, and personality, that does not make one independent from the community. Individual uniqueness, personality, and ambitions are meaningful only when seen in the framework of the whole. As Benjamin Ray (1976, 33) writes,

> African views of a human seek a balance between one of collective identity as a member of society and one of personal identity as a unique individual. African thinking defines people in terms of the social groups to which they belong. A person is thought of first of all as a constituent of a particular community, for it is the community which defines who one is and what one can become.

He continues, speaking of Western ideas of individual freedom:

> The traditional African is too systematic for such a doctrine, too logical and dynamically integrated. Destiny and community always balance freedom and individuality, and these in turn are balanced by natural and supernatural powers. Each person is a nexus of interesting elements of the self and of

the world, which shape and are shaped
by one's behavior.

The depth of the collective identity is why
individual, long-range goals are difficult to realize in
terms of traditional life. In the village, day to day
living is the common concern, centered on the
mothers. An individual in traditional, communal
society never exists in terms of "I," the subjective part,
but always in terms of "we," the collective part. The
collective part far overshadows the subjective.

There are advantages and disadvantages to this
integration. On the plus side, it rescues the "have-nots"
from worry, anxiety, helplessness, hopelessness, and a
lack of confidence. A person is never alienated from
oneself or others, for alienation is something that
occurs in a society where individualism is the norm.
On the negative side, it does not allow one to progress
or to accumulate a great deal of wealth. To keep wealth
without sharing it is considered inhuman in the Nilotic
community. Sharing is one of the key mechanisms for
welding and constructing the community, and it
affirms some of the community's basic beliefs about
human relations.

Another negative is that there are no secrets in
the community. For example, a person stealing or
committing adultery acts alone, but the burden of this
action is shared by all. The community support of a
wrongdoer, however, does not mean approval of his or
her actions. If someone has injured another, justice
must then be carried out. The Nilotic people believe in
social order and in the observance of the law. Although
their laws are not written down, they are universal and
perfectly known. The law is the custom. It is that
which has always been done. It is what is best for the

whole group, and what is best for everyone. In both good times and in bad times, the community's good spirit prevails.

The African in general, and Nilotic people in particular, live not in the shadow of what one has, but rather in the light of what one is. This is the African formula of one being, in both nature and in community. In contrast to the West, where a person's property—house, car, clothes, money, and even children—are considered as much a part of the private self as is one's own body, in Africa a person's property is considered a part of the community.

These fundamental cultural differences explain in part why not all parents in Akot saw the value of exposing their children to Western education. Some were concerned about the potentially damaging effects that Western ideas would have on the family. They saw this education as destroying the children. They really did not know anything about schooling. Because it was a new thing, they suspected that something might be wrong with it.

I was caught on the bridge between the traditional and the modern ways of life. My choice was to move forward, as my father did, trying to learn as much as I could. Many children like me who attended school in Africa became outsiders within their own culture. The traditional people felt that the educated people did not respect their elders. Resentment and misunderstanding sometimes resulted when the educated ones expressed thoughts or behaved differently than the other community members. As Ngugi wa Thiong'o (1974, 32) explains:

> The first education given was merely to
> enable converts to read the Bible, so

that they could carry out simple duties as assistants to the missionaries. As education later came to be the ladder to better jobs and money (material wealth) and to higher standard of living, albeit in the image of the European mode of life, the Christian-educated African became even more removed from his or her ancestral shrines and roots.

Western education not only contributed to the unattractiveness of rural life, but also further encouraged young men and women to search for new opportunities and different ways of life. European culture and religion attracted away from the village some of the best and brightest young people, and assured the death of the Nilotic traditions and the self-alienation and communal exclusion of the newly educated.

Accepting the Christian church often meant the outright rejection of African customs. It meant rejection of those values and rituals that held the Nilotic people together. It meant adapting what in effect was a European middle-class mode of living and behavior. The European missionaries attacked the rites of the Nilotic people, condemning the images of our gods and our beautiful African dances, recoiling from their sensuality. The early Nilotic converts followed this lead, often with even greater zeal, for they had to prove how Christian they were through the rejection of their cultural roots.

Many other Africans besides my sisters and me suffered as victims of these radical cultural changes. Our entire village was distressed and my father sharply criticized for sending us girls to a school to be raised by the kind of women who discouraged family life. Everyone thought my father a madman because he sent his three daughters away to school. People told him that he was throwing away his future because we would grow up learning the ways of the white nuns, who did not marry because they thought they were the brides of God's son.

The unmarried status of the priests and nuns was seen as something of a joke by the Dinka, because to them there was no life without marriage. They would always ask the nuns and priests why they did not want to get married. Refusing to marry was considered immoral in the Dinka community. It was an approval of prostitution. The Dinka think that every man and woman must get married, because if they do not reproduce, the older people will die and that will be the end of the world. The Dinka told the nuns and priests that the God they knew created man and woman so that they could have life together, produce children, and continue life upon the earth.

My own sense of individuality and ambition emerged to a greater extent as I received more exposure to learning and the environment outside of my immediate culture. One day in the lecture hall at the intermediate school in Wau, a middle-aged Arab woman spoke to our senior class. She praised the school system for having given her a good education, leading her to personal satisfaction and a leadership role. I discovered that the woman was valedictorian of her graduating class. She had graduated from Umdurman High School in northern Sudan, attended the University of Khartoum, and was now the first woman to work in the Ministry of Education. Nothing else before this had made such a profound impression on me. If this woman could be at the head of her class, surely I could attain something similar.

It was during this period, the mid to late 1960s, that more Nilotic families began changing their attitudes about education. This was because they were coming to regard it a weapon that could empower all Africans in their fight against colonialism. The ability to speak the English language and to communicate, for example, was quickly seen as an advantage to families fighting the tax system of the colonial administration.

In 1967, the growing civil war in the South captured the attention of many young people. Students began protesting all over the South. Some students, especially the boys, refused to take Islamic Studies classes and left to join the southern rebel army, which was known as the *Anya- Anya*, or Snake Venom. I wasted no time in anger over political developments.

I studied hard in my classes and passed them all with high grades. I was on the right track.

October 21, 1972
Julia and Wal during the church ceremony.

Chapter IV

Marriage

A young African girl becomes a mother before she is a woman. She is taught to be good, to be obedient, and to do what her mother tells her. In the Nilotic tradition, marriage is a round and complete circle indicating the wholeness and oneness of the relationship which is being entered into. There is no separation and fragmentation, but a complete relationship which offers fullness and completeness to each partner, family, clan, and society as whole.

What do I Know About Marriage?

When I was young, all I knew about the institution of marriage was that people grew up and they got married. I never imagined how much was involved in marriage. The relentless cage of routine and rote. It is not only cooking meals everyday, but also getting to know other people and their backgrounds. It is understanding the lives of other people, especially that of your husband, and it is raising your children to become responsible adults. If I could start all over again, I would ask my father to give me five more years of training to prepare me for this most important role in society, especially for the big responsibility of raising and protecting my children.

In marriage, the role of parenting is a lifetime responsibility, one believed by the Nilotic people to be very important for both genders, but especially for females. There are certain desirable parental qualities, but the Nilotic people generally say that mothers are to possess such qualities to greater degrees than are fathers. Of these are the capacity to be courageous and to have pity and understanding. A Nilotic mother should also be able to endure suffering and hardship without complaint. In this she sets an example for her children. This quality is especially critical to the ordeal of childbirth. If a woman is not brave during childbirth, for example, her reputation suffers.

A Nilotic mother is expected to forgive and forget after she has had a hard dispute with someone. She must be able to maintain amicable relations in spite of any differences within the extended family. All these qualities are symbolically associated with the role of motherhood.

Marriage as an institution serves in every society to bring men and women together into an exclusive and enduring relationship. Marriage among the Nilotic also brings people into important relationships with in-laws. Social science scholars argue that marriage is a convenient means for providing a division of labor between male and female. Each person contributes talents and capabilities to the economy of the family. These scholars also reason that the family is an economic essential, providing for the sustenance of the dependent young and forming, at the same time, the setting for their socialization. I can say this from my own marriage experience that these observations are true.

In many societies the family is the primary group, integral to the domestic economy and paramount in child rearing. Nilotic families are organized according to the rules surrounding corporate property and the behavioral requirements of producing a livelihood. The family provides the entire framework of interpersonal relationships and is essential to the formation, as well as to the connectedness, of its members. The marriage of one's mother and father gives the individual a rounded and full spectrum of relatives. Among the Nilotic people, clan membership derives from the patrilineal descent, providing one part of an individual's total kinship network. The network extends beyond the patrilineal clan through the mother's relatives. It extends further to the relatives of a person's spouse and to the relatives of the children of the union when they marry as well. Marriage and blood are the great social glue of the Nilotic society. In this case, marriage and kinship are more than a conventional means of reaching a useful end; they are also the basic criteria and conceptual bases for the division of society into its parts and for the re-amalgamation of these parts into a whole.

The Nilotic people believe that marriages are arranged by God. The initial assumption is that marriage is the happy enactment of divine will and that it is destined to endure forever in this world. A Nilotic always expects to have a good marital life. The continuation of a patrilineal society depends upon its males, so the traditions surrounding marriage are of key importance. Marriage arrangements epitomize the basic principle of the Nilotic society. In order to serve the well being of society as a whole, all matters such as bridewealth must be patiently and peacefully negotiated. This is to avoid broken families and to ensure stable families.

My Marriage

After attending school for four years in Wau and graduating from the intermediate level, I enrolled in 1971 at Wad Medani Teachers Training College in northern Sudan. Girls from all over the country and from all sorts of backgrounds attended this college. I began college during the years of socialist government, a period in which the Sudanese system of education was open to all citizens regardless of sex, religion, or birthplace.

The socialist educational system began introducing the concept of ethnic and cultural diversity. As I explored the great variety of perspectives inside and outside the college setting, I gradually became aware that Sudan as a nation had a long way to go before it could attain the status of more developed countries. I spent two years studying at Wad Medani, and in 1972 graduated with the Sudan Teaching Certificate.

At sixteen, I was still running among the young women, still young, innocent, and free. I wanted to experience life deeply. I wanted to have a career, to teach for few years, to save some money, and to travel. I wanted to be free—free to know people and their backgrounds, free to move to different parts of the world. But I was never so blinded by this youthful ambition that I could not see my share of existence within my family. Unknown to me, however, while I was finishing my studies at Wad Medani my share of existence within my family was an important topic of discussion.

In August of 1972, during the wet season, my father called one of my sisters and me to talk. We had just finished our teachers' training and were posted to teach in the local school in Wau town where our family lived at that time. My sister and I were hoping to take a trip to Port Sudan to see the Red Sea during the coming dry season when schools were closed. My father told us to sit and we did. He had just returned from visiting my older brother who was working as a doctor in Omdurman Hospital in Khartoum. My father said, "Your brother Dr. Marial would like for you girls to visit him this summer." We both jumped up happily and said, "Yes, that would fit our plans. We will go to Khartoum and from there to Port Sudan."

But before we could continue our celebrations, my father cleared his throat and said, "Something new has come up. I want to tell you about my recent visit to Khartoum. One of you will get married. There is a young man from my home village who has just came back from the United States of America. He is now working for the Regional government in Juba. He is a gentle man, so he will be kind to his wife. He will come soon to visit and to meet you and your mothers. His name is Michael Wal Duany. He had asked to marry into our family. He proposed to marry Nyakal (Julia)."

A chill passed from my head, down my spine, and to my feet. I wanted to hold on to something but I could not find anything. The only thing I could hold on to was my clothing. I hugged my clothes close to me at this difficult moment.

I did not say a word. In Nilotic culture, a father's decision was not to be questioned by a good daughter. During youth, a Nilotic girl was exposed to certain facts of life. She was to honor her parents. She must have proper posture and good manners in all she does. When my father and my two older bothers Marial and Maker met with Wal and his relatives, they

115

accepted their proposal and agreed to settle the marriage because they expected me to accept their decision. I had to respect my family's decision. The men even went so far as to set the wedding day, October 21, 1972. The rest of my family—my mother, my four stepmothers, and everyone else—were informed later.

My sister was very proud that I was getting married. I was not sure what I was getting into. I had my own dreams of going for further education. I wanted to be free. I wanted to venture out into what people so fancifully called civilized life. I wanted to be a free woman, but I had to obey my father. And that meant accepting the marriage.

In Nilotic culture, a young woman does not take the initiative in proposing marriage. This is the responsibility of the young man in concert with his cousins. It is assumed that a young man will marry when he is old enough to take on responsibility for the lives of others. A suitable wife must then be found for him.

The bridegroom does not search for a wife or approach a woman on his own. If he meets someone he would particularly like to be his future wife, he first has to tell his cousins of the same age to approach the young woman to see if she is interested in him. If the cousins come back with a positive response, then the young man must talk to his paternal uncle, who is respected in the family for decency and mature judgment. The bridegroom then announces that he is ready to start a family. The elders in the family must be convinced that the young man is able to look after himself. He should be able to build his own house, work steadily, and feed not only his wife and children, but also contribute to the well-being of the extended family. Before proceeding any further the young man must make a successful case for himself and obtain the agreement and support of his relatives.

After this initial requirement has been met, it is the task of the elders of the bridegroom to let everyone know that the young man has an interest in marrying and to ask relatives, those of his age, to search for a decent girl. Often the young man does not have a woman in mind, so the relatives must make inquiries to find someone suitable. In either case, when the relatives settle on a prospective wife, the uncle talks to a reputable man of the bride's family, seeking his advice. When this uncle has been convinced that the woman would make a desirable wife for his brother's son, he returns to his relatives to discuss the matter in detail. When the family members are satisfied with the potential union, a visit will be made to the future wife's family with a formal request for marriage. Before a family can give consent to a marriage, long discussions must be held in which each family considers the other's history and background. If both families agree to the marriage, a date for the ceremony will be set. Although Nilotic marriages are arranged, the belief is that no one should be forced into marriage against his or her will. The family does make inquiry about whether the two young people like each other. This was how my marriage came about. Two families agreed to become related through the union of a son and daughter.

A universal feature of traditional African marriage is the provision of brideweath. Bridewealth means uniting the two families into one lineage through the sharing of both substance and persons. The bride's family sets the bridewealth to be received from the groom's family. Every member of the groom's family is expected to contribute cattle to make up the bridewealth. Uncles and aunts from both the groom's maternal and paternal families contribute their share of cattle.

Among the Nilotic marriage involves the exchange of a significant amount of property. Among the Nuer communities the amount of the bridewealth, in some cases, may go up to twenty or thirty head of cattle. Among the Dinka communities the amount is higher, anywhere from sixty to more than a hundred head of cattle. In the traditional marriage ceremony, the young husband places an Ivory bracelet on his wife's left wrist as a token of his trusting her with his property and life. This is the ritual of marriage; the families, rather than the individuals, are the players.

Traditional wedding ceremonies are performed during the harvest time when there is enough food. The wedding is a grand, happy event attracting people from all over the surrounding area. Members of the immediate family come to the wedding from great distances. The ceremony begins with the pouring of *cak, kong,* and *pii* (milk, wine, and water) on the ground to welcome the ancestors. Prayers are said to the Creator *(Kuoth).* This sets the proper upbeat, joyous tone for the proceedings. The women on the bridegroom's side dance and sing songs praising the family members. The men kill a bull or bulls as a symbol of unity among the two families. The blood of the bull symbolizes the mixture of the human bloodlines through which children are born. After the ancestors have been addressed, each family's spokesman comes forward in turn to present his prayers. These spokesmen are always chosen from among the elders of the families, men that are considered wise and worthy of respect.

The Day I Met Wal

I now waited for the inevitable day when Wal Duany would come to visit us. One day we received a telegram. My father gave it to me. I read it and passed it to my sister, who read it and gave it back to my father. Wal was coming.

My sister and I left the room. We went out and sat under the tree to talk. I was afraid.

"I do not know what to do. I do not want to be married now," I said to my sister.

"He may be a nice person and you may like him. Please wait and see who this guy is," she said.

"I want to know the person I am going to marry," I said in a shaking voice. "This marriage is just like a dream in my sleep except that when I wake up it will all be true."

"Give yourself some time to think it over. You never know," my sister said, "something good could come out of this. Look at the positive side. If our father and brothers accept this man, then he must be a good person. He loves you, that is why he spoke to our family."

"How can he love somebody he never saw? He never spoke with me or wrote to me or sent one of his cousins to talk to me. Everyone says he is a good man, but how do I know?" I was angry and did not want to talk with my sister any more.

I went to visit my brother's girlfriend Rosezanna Acol. I liked her because she was a very broad-minded woman. I knocked at the door and her little girl answered. "Mama, it is Julia," she yelled. I walked straight into the living room, looking sad. Acol was usually a very lively person. I always enjoyed her

119

company. She came from the kitchen with a towel in her hands, swinging her hips and dancing. With a loud voice, she sang a song in Swahili, "Here comes the bride, ta, ta, ta, ta! *Malaika, nakupeneda Malaika!* Angel, I love you Angel!"

I smiled a little and said softly, "Hey, hey, hey, stop it. Stop it, please. I am here to hide, not to celebrate. You do not know how I feel."

"*AA wii* (an Egyptian word for please)! I understand your feelings. My Doc (that was what she called my brother) called yesterday to tell me the good news. He is excited about coming to the wedding. We are all happy for you. I met Wal when I was in Khartoum. He is a nice person. Many of the women are running after him! You better not say no." She broke out in loud laughter. Her neighbor overheard our conversation and joined in. There was no place to hide in Wau town! Everywhere I went, people asked me about the marriage. I told them politely, "I don't know. I have not met this man yet."

On a Friday afternoon we saw the commissioner's car, conspicuous as the only white Mercedes in town, coming toward our house. Everyone stood up to look at the car as it slowed and stopped in front of our house. The people thought that *bany diit* (the big man) of the town was in it. But there were no passengers, only the driver, who gave my father a note. The note was to inform my father that Wal had arrived in town and would come to our house in the evening. He was staying in the government guesthouse.

That afternoon everyone in my family put on their best clothes. My sister, my two friends, and I all dressed in our very nicest dresses and sat in our room, waiting for the gentleman caller to arrive. At 4:00 p.m. Wal arrived at our house. His cousin, Stephen Ciec

Lam, who was seven feet tall, accompanied him. People were excited because they thought that Stephen Ciec was the bridegroom. The Nilotic people admire height because they consider it to be beautiful.

The guests sat in the living room with my father. Everyone in my family went to meet them. My sister, my two girlfriends and I were the last to meet them. When it was our turn, I had a funny feeling. I was afraid, but I had to show courage in facing these men. We entered the living room, which now seemed too small for me. We greeted Wal and Stephen and sat down. I chose a chair near the door, as if I might run off if anything happened.

I saw right away that Wal was a gentleman. He was dressed handsomely in a beautiful navy blue suit. I had expected to see a sluggish man with a potbelly. This fear took shape because I had been told that Wal had been to the United States. In rural Sudan, people who have never been outside the country have stereotypes about people who live in industrialized countries. They picture these people as being fat. This image is associated with good living, a lot of food, and material wealth, but it is not attractive.

With a smile on his face Wal said, "I have come to take you girls back to Nuer land. I want to take Julia home." I was speechless, but my sister, who was our spokeswoman replied, "That is a good idea. We would be glad to go home with you. We have been waiting for this moment all of our lives." That was the statement of acceptance.

I was frozen. I thought I might faint. These two strange men were looking right at me, and here my sister with her quick mouth had accepted the marriage. At that moment I knew the marriage was set, because everyone admired Wal. I simply could not come out and say that I did not want to be married now. Everyone in my family would think I was being insensitive. Slowly, I began to think. Every member of my family wished me the best. I had to trust my family. I also had to convince myself that I was not the first woman to be married. Many Nilotic women before me had gone through this process. My family would not do something to hurt me. I knew that I could count on them, and that they would be there for me if I ever should need them. They would all be on my side if anything happened. As I looked about me, it really was nice to see every member of my family so happy to be a part of this relationship.

It had always been my father's wish that someone from his home village would marry one of his daughters. That way, my father would have someone to take him home. The day Wal visited our home was the day my father's dream came true. I had never seen my father so happy. The Lord had made his day, because someone from his home village had come to ask his daughter for marriage.

The visit lasted into the evening. The conversation was dominated by politics. We all tried to avoid directly discussing the subject of marriage. The men talked about peace and the recent Addis Ababa Agreement between the southern rebels and the Sudanese government. We all debated its implications for the South. The evening ended nicely. We had a good time because all of us were interested in politics.

The Nuer have a saying, "Talking with one another is loving one another." From that day forward, I began to learn that love is something one has to grow into. It is a process that one has to take step by step, gradually getting to know one another and developing trust and respect for one another. My people were right; it takes time to learn to love.

After three decades, I am still in my marriage. Both Wal and I have learned how to communicate, to open our minds and hearts, to accept new possibilities, new alternatives, new options. I credit my husband Wal, because he made it possible for me to have an inward sense of excitement, security, and adventure, and to believe that our lives would be significantly better together than they were before.

The Wedding Days

My family began the marriage celebration two months before the ceremony. I was given bedding, two big bottles of perfume, and a bucket full of ready-made sandal oil. Traditionally, new brides use sandal oil in order to smell good. My mother went shopping to buy kitchen supplies and many other goods for my new household. My older sister Martha Apanda prepared three hundred kilos of dried meat, a two by two foot square tin of peanut butter, and twenty-five pounds of dried okra. All of this food was to go home with me after the wedding.

Our home also was busy for two months entertaining the many visitors who came to feast. Old women sang and danced all day. Two sheep were slaughtered every day to feed all the guests. The old people drank *marisa,* a local beer made of sorghum. The Nilotic do not drink a lot of beer, except during celebrations and ceremonies like weddings. These are opportunities for the old people to have some beer and a good time. These are also times when older women recall their own weddings and tell their stories.

My younger stepmother Anguaj was the wedding coordinator. She took care of all the visitors. I was relieved of all my domestic duties and had to stay indoors until the day of my wedding. This was because I had to go through all of the marriage rituals. One important ritual was the skin treatment. I had to endure this treatment twice a day. I hated this part of the preparation. A bride has to remove all skin flakes and hair from all parts of her body, except for the hair on her head. I struggled with my stepmother and brother's girlfriend Acol because the treatment burned my skin.

These harsh skin treatments are customs that women from the South have adopted from the northern Sudanese. The traditional skin treatment of the Nilotic people is simple. One applies oil (melted butter) to the bride's skin three times a day and bathes in warm water. This makes the skin shiny and smooth. The northern Sudanese women use sesame oil mixed with sandalwood oil, plus many other perfumes, which make the skin smell very strong. To achieve this saturation, a pit is dug in the ground and a fire is prepared in it. A platform with a hole in the middle is placed over the fire pit. After all hair had been removed, the bride's body is oiled and perfumed. She then sits on the platform above the fire. The women burn acacia wood, which generates a lot of smoke. The bride covers her body with a blanket to trap the smoke, leaving her head out for breathing. The smoke smells strong of sandalwood and turns the skin yellowish and shiny.

I endured this procedure every morning and evening, sitting for three hours at a time with the fire right at my feet and my body bundled up in a thick blanket. Sitting above the fire generates a lot of sweat, which smoothes the body. When this treatment is repeated many times and done well, it gives a smooth touch and glowing tone to the skin. This was the same idea as skin tanning, which now is a popular beauty treatment among women in the United States.

I was allowed to go out of the house only after sundown. When I wanted to go somewhere, my stepmother and my sisters accompanied me. I spent two long months indoors. Relatives came to visit. Older women came to give me their blessing. They all kissed my hands and poured cold water on my feet and hands and sprinkled my stomach. This was a sign of wishing peace and harmony for the new family. They said their words of advice, and told me how to behave, and how to treat my husband and my in-laws. Although these women stressed respect and trust for my husband, they also gave very strong advice about sexual relationships.

In the Nilotic culture, sexual intercourse is avoided during the time a woman is menstruating. Cleanliness is one of the traits a woman is expected to observe. The older women told me that I must not meet with my husband during this period. They also cautioned that intercourse during pregnancy could cause miscarriage, defects, or even the death of the mother. The women said that if the whiteness of the semen came in contact with the baby's head, it could cause a skin condition characterized by light-colored spots of pigmentation. Semen could cause the water in the womb to thicken, making delivery difficult. If a child were born with these spots, it would be assumed that the parents had violated the rule against intercourse during pregnancy. If during one's first delivery the midwife suspects that there has been intercourse during the pregnancy, the mother's reputation suffers. It also means that no midwife will deliver her subsequent babies, because she is considered dirty and sinful. Femininity is defined as having in full measure the cultural traits most valued by the Nilotic society. Women are supposed to have a greater tendency to be clean and neat in their personal habits than are men; to be otherwise is a greater disgrace for a woman than it is for a man.

The Nilotic people believe that every married woman has the right to bear children. This is why the older women teach the young women all of the rules guiding marriage. For example, the bride must be told of the danger of having sex before her wedding day. She must learn to protect herself from early sexual relations and must be courageous to meet her husband when the time comes. All young women feared the possibility of barrenness as well as the trial of the first intercourse. The older women monitored the result of the first intercourse of the marriage. If the bride had engaged in pre-marital sexual relations, it would show.

Young women no longer observe these traditional customs. Nowadays, some young women engage in sexual relationships before marriage. They think tradition does not hold with what they have learned of modern ways. Many of these young women, especially the educated ones who have studied and read about birth control, believe they know more than their parents did.

Among the Nilotic, childbirth is a cause for celebration. It is likened to death, and new mothers are visited and given presents to congratulate them for escaping the throes of death. A woman is given special delicacies, such as fish, liver, chicken soup and warm milk, to help with her recuperation. It is customary for a woman to have a sister or other female relative come and assist her during the last weeks of pregnancy and for some weeks after childbirth. In the Nilotic culture, a woman's good health is vital, and the wisdom of taking time away from hard work after the delivery to recuperate is recognized. The Nilotic believe that women's health is important for reproduction. A healthy woman is able to have children easier than a woman who is not healthy. So, providing the mother-to-be with sufficient rest and nutritious foods becomes the responsibility of the husband. His hunting and fishing activities must increase.

Reproductive health is taken seriously by women. Mothers worry when their daughters' first menstruation is delayed or if their menstrual intervals seem irregular. Women who have problems conceiving or who suffer frequent miscarriages invest a lot of time and money in visiting "diviner herbalists." Herbalists administer herbs gathered from home gardens, the fields, or the forest. Pregnant women constantly drink and bathe in herbs that protect the baby's health and make delivery easier. Now, with modern medicines, medical services are becoming more accessible to women and this has contributed to better reproductive health.

The Church Ceremony

Following the traditional wedding preparations came the day of wearing the white dress in the church. In Wau town, the majority of people were Catholics. Their church was very big. I was not married there, but in the Episcopal Church. This was a small, old church built by the British commissioner and his family during the early 1900s. Everything in the church was worn out. The walls, floor, windows, doors, and even the altar were in bad shape.

Wal and my father went to see the church and talk to the pastor. Pastor John Malou Ater was the minister at the time. When Wal offered to send some people to fix up the church, it was a Godsend. A whole army unit was sent to do the work. A week later the old church looked new. The soldiers replaced the windows and covered the floor with new carpet. They painted the walls and installed electric ceiling fans. This little congregation had no money to cover all these improvements. The members of the church thought it was a miracle for something as good as this could happen to their church.

Our wedding day, October 21, 1972, also was a big day for the new Regional Government, established by the Addis Ababa Agreement. Wal was in charge of the national military integration program. This program was for training and integrating the southern Sudanese freedom fighters into the national army. The first group, after finishing six months of training, was to graduate that day.

The President of the Republic of Sudan His Excellency Gaafar Mohammed Nimeiry, Vice Presidents His Excellency Abel Alier and His Excellency Abul Gassim Mohammed Ibrahim, and many dignitaries in the central and regional governments were in town for the graduation and to attend our wedding. The graduation ceremony took place at the church in the morning and our wedding took place in the evening. Vice President His Excellency Abul Gassim Mohammed Ibrahim was Wal's best man.

The events of the day united Sudanese from all regions and walks of life. Muslims and Christians sat together in the church, which was packed. Many people in Wau town attended the wedding. There were people everywhere. I will never forget that day because it symbolized the possibility of peace and unity in our nation. It was a lesson to be learned by all Sudanese that we can live together regardless of our differences.

At 8:00pm, after the church ceremony, we went to the commissioner's house for a big dinner party. Five bulls and twenty-five sheep were slaughtered for the party. There were plenty of drinks, both home-brewed beer and market beer, as well as soft drinks. The party lasted the whole night, but I could not keep up with everyone because I was very tired. At 10:00 p.m., I left the party and was taken to the guesthouse where Wal and I were to spend the night. Once I left the party, I became frightened. I begged my sister and my stepmother not to leave me alone in the room. They assured me that my fears were normal. Every woman had to go through this ritual and it would be all right.

In the morning, I did not want to be seen by anyone. I did not want to face anyone I knew. This was the most difficult part of my wedding. I was embarrassed and did not want people to look at me. I was ashamed and wanted to hide my face. My sister and my stepmother came to collect the bedding before Wal and I left the guesthouse. It is a tradition that the mother should wash (and inspect) the bedding of her daughter's first marriage night. I was thankful that Wal and I were leaving town the next day, because I did not want to see the old ladies celebrate, although I had proved to them that I had been a good girl.

We left the following morning for Khartoum where Wal attended a meeting with the United States Agency International for Development (USAID). We spent a week in Khartoum, but it was all business. We did not have a honeymoon afterwards because we both had to work. Schools were opening and I was scheduled to teach. In the Nilotic culture, the bride is given a long honeymoon. Her husband and in-laws provide all services until she has her first baby. I did not enjoy that custom.

After one week of work in Khartoum, we arrived in Juba at noon on October 30, 1972. We lived for two months in the government guesthouse, and then we were allotted a house. It was an old house that needed a lot of work. I made all of the curtains, because there were no ready-made ones available. My father sent my three sisters, Monica Acol, Helen Atoma, and Margaret Aliu to help me put my house in order. I also had help from my friends and my uncle's wife Fowzia Belal who lived in town. It took us three weeks to put the house in order. Then Wal and I settled down to married life.

Marriage ended my dream of traveling the world. That's what I thought. But my dream of travel came true. Whenever I was not teaching, I accompanied Wal on business trips, both in the country and abroad. I never get tired of going on trips. New places excited me and added to my knowledge of history and geography. Some of my first trips were to Addis Ababa, Ethiopia; Geneva, Switzerland; Rome, Italy; and London, England. These excursions enabled me to experience Western civilization first hand, and to fill in many of the missing pieces of what I had learned in school. I never knew, for instance, that some English people were poor and lived on the streets.

It was also a surprise to meet English or European men and women who were friendly and trustworthy. When Wal went to business meetings in London, his English friends took me sightseeing. It was only as I had close contact with English people in their own homeland that I was able to overcome my prejudice against them. The English people I met were kind and treated us with respect. I did not understand why they behaved so differently when they were in Africa.

Through my exposure to other peoples and cultures, I began to understand that people are people no matter what color they are or where they live. They can be evil or they can be good. To overcome prejudice one must be ready to learn and willing to meet, trust, and respect others. It was as Vincent Ostrom, my professor at Indiana University, would later often repeat, "we just have to learn from one another."

Becoming a Mother

The trips ended when I became sick one morning. I felt troubled the whole day. My stomach was upset and I thought that I had stomach flu. The next day I was sick again in the morning. I could not hold any food in my stomach. I went to see our family doctor, who promptly congratulated me on my first pregnancy.

My uncle's wife Fozzia Belal was very happy. The next day she visited all our relatives and friends to give them the good news and invite them to a celebration. She went shopping and bought all kind of foods. We slaughtered two sheep and everybody feasted. I was to be a mother, and that was cause for everyone to celebrate.

Our first child Urom was born on March 10, 1974, at St. Mary Hospital in Khartoum. The hospital is known by many Sudanese women as *Rhabbat,* the Sisters. Urom was a born a healthy baby, showing no sign of weakness.

One night in Juba when Urom was seventeen months old he had a very high fever. I gave him children's aspirin and the fever came down. In two hours the fever was up again. Wal was in Khartoum on a business trip. I awakened my mother, who was visiting, and told her the baby was sick. We sat up the whole night trying to reduce the fever. We used warm and cold water compresses to bring down Urom's temperature but that did not help him at all.

In the morning, the fever was even higher. We took the baby to the hospital where he was admitted. The doctor confirmed our suspicions. It was typhoid fever. I prayed for a miracle, that Urom would recover. In developing countries, children are the most likely to be infected with typhoid and dysentery because they are the least likely to have immunity from earlier exposure. They are the most likely to die.

Urom spent two nights in the hospital, but he did not improve. The doctors did all they could to control the raging fever, but his body never responded to any treatment. At 10:00 a.m., on April 17, 1975, my seventeen-month old boy slipped into a coma. I knew then that it was over.

I was devastated. He was my first child. I felt as if most of myself had passed away with him. He was healthy. He had never gotten sick, as most babies do. I found it hard to accept that I lost him, even when I tearfully kissed him goodbye and then covered his face with a sheet. When the coffin lid was closed, two men screwed it down. I could still see Urom's face in that closed box. The first night I spent without him was long. I heard the clock in the hall striking. I counted the beats, sitting in the intense silence, knowing I would never see my baby again. People told me that as a Christian I should thank God because my baby was now an angel in heaven. But I had lost my little baby, who I carried in my body for nine months and gave birth to after a long night of pain. My heart was broken. No one understood how I felt.

When I think about it to this day, I shut my eyes and try to blot out the awful truth. It is hard to let go of loved ones. After twenty-four years, that pain is till fresh in my heart. The anguish is awful. My baby was my world. He was seldom absent from my thoughts. He was an angelic baby, but now he is gone.

After Urom's death, Wal and I had to pick up the pieces and go about the business of living. I soon was pregnant with our second child. Duany, our second son, was born on November 2, 1976 at a hospital in Juba. We named him Duany, which is Wal's family name.

In time, four more children were born to us. Our five children, Duany, Nyagon, Kueth, Nok, and Bil, have been constant sources of comfort and inspiration. Without these children, I do not know what my life would be. The time I spent raising my children were moments of nurturing. They are grown now, and as I let them go, I trust that I have prepared them and given them skills for life. I want them to know that I am there for them. They must understand that Mom is the "custodian of life."

Wal Duany, Ph.D, May 1992
Nyagon, Wal, Julia, Duany, Nok
Kueth, Bil

Chapter V

Things Fall Apart

Every time I think of my homeland, I
hold back my tears and pretend like I
am okay with my departure.

Leaving Africa

One summer evening in August of 1983, Wal
was sitting in the living room of our house in Juba.
There was tension in the city. The radio had just
announced that the Sudan Peoples Liberation
Army/Movement (SPLA/M) had attacked and killed
many people in Joku, one of the small towns at the
Ethiopian border in the Upper Nile Region. Civil war
was breaking out. Wal got up from where he was
sitting and picked up a book from our small library. He
sat down on the sofa and opened the book, but did not
read it. He just held it on his lap. Earlier that day, the
government had ordered all former and present
southern government officials to report to the national
security office. Wal had reported that afternoon. He
was told not to go anywhere without first informing the
authorities.

As Wal sat thinking, there was a knock on the
front door. He opened the door and three young men
walked in. They were Juba University students, Wal's
nephews Gat Luak, Gat Lou, and Gat Kuoth. I greeted
the young men and brought tea. When I brought the tea
and knelt down to pour, Wal and the three young men

seemed not to notice. I told them that the tea was ready and turned to go to the kitchen to get some donuts, but when I heard what they were saying, I stopped. These young men were telling Wal to leave Juba. They said it was not safe anymore for people like him. I was shaken by the warning, even though I had seen it coming.

A year earlier, involved with my young family, I did not want to imagine that my happiness might come to an end. My house in Juba was my happy world. I especially loved the kitchen. I loved making tea, preferring to prepare it myself even in the daytime when I had help from the housegirl, because the kitchen was my world. My husband and sons never entered that part of the house. The kitchen gave me authority and power within the household.

Yet by 1983, my world had come crashing down. From the creation of the southern regional government in 1972 until he lost his position in 1982, Wal served as a government minister. Although the regional government was abolished once and for all in September 1983, President Nimeiry had been dismantling it by degrees since 1980. In the process, Wal became a political target and was held in jail for a year without trial. That injustice was hard enough on our family, but worse, we could see that Khartoum's treachery was transforming the entire Republic of Sudan into a centrally governed Islamic state.

Actually, it was going to get a lot worse. In September 1983, all citizens of Sudan fell under the jurisdiction of the *Shari'a,* Islamic law. This meant that as a Christian family, the Duany family had no civil rights.

That evening in August 1983, as I stood listening to Wal and his nephews talk, I heard the loud siren of a police car pass by. I thought, "It's time to leave Juba." I looked into Wal's eyes, but he avoided mine and kept talking. One of our neighbors walked in and joined the conversation. Tears filled my eyes and I was not able to speak. I turned away because I did not want to cry in front of these men.

"Why is all this happening?" I thought bitterly. "Why is it that southern Sudanese have to leave the country, go to jail, or die?" While the men talked, I walked through the house, picking up things and putting things in order. I did not know what to take or what to leave. I enjoyed keeping my house spotlessly clean. I loved this house and I did not want to leave it. Life here was an adventure because I could make it beautiful.

Wal was not happy either. He did not want to leave the country. During the first civil war in the 1960s he had lived in exile. He spent his adolescence living in the jungles of southern Sudan as a member of the Southern Sudan Liberation Movement (SSLM), known as *Anya-Anya*. It was the first movement organized by the southern Sudanese to fight against the Islamic-dominated government. Wal was one of the young men chosen by the movement to obtain a higher education. He spent five more years away from home as a student in the United States of America. I knew he would not be happy to live in exile again. Nevertheless, I made a resolution that night.

After the men left I opened my heart and talked to Wal. I told him that we would have to leave Juba. My hands were shaking. He held my hands and asked, "Where do you want to go?"

"To the United States," I said. "Don't you have friends there?"

"Of course I do," he replied.

"I don't want to go to Kenya or to the United Kingdom or to any African country," I said.

"Go to bed," Wal answered. "We will think about it together."

That night we did not sleep at all. We were as restless as cattle in the camp when the mosquitoes attack at night. Our worried tossing sounded like the fast movement of the animals' swatting tails. In my mind, I went over my reasons for choosing the United States.

London was not an option. In 1982, I had gone to London to visit my brother Barnaba Marial, a medical doctor. There, I had seen many other Sudanese professionals who were living as refugees. As I visited these families, I heard the same story again and again. They were all living on welfare. The children were not exposed to real life and were growing up with no discipline and no morality. The welfare system seemed to encourage families to break up. Women were given support if they left their husbands. The Sudanese in London were now numbers in the British Home Office books. They were being fed to death by the welfare state. Some weighed over 200 pounds and had grown large potbellies.

When I looked at the refugee situation in Africa it too seemed hopeless. The basic social, economic, and political problems were overwhelming, even without the refugee crisis. Refugees need food, shelter, healthcare, education, and employment, none of which were easily obtained in Africa. Remaining on the continent was not a solution for us.

I wanted a place where I could have stability, where my children could go to school, and where Wal and I could find some work to provide a living for ourselves. Generation after generation of southern

Sudanese women had struggled to raise families, overcome illiteracy, powerlessness, and abuses. Their courage was with me, yet moving to America was a new challenge.

Although I wanted to go to America, I was also afraid because of what I believed was happening—stolen or lost children, child abuse, rape, killing on the streets, drug addition, alcoholism, homosexuality, and racism. I had read American books and seen American movies and now nightmarish scenes ran through my mind. As I lay staring at the ceiling, I felt that I was gambling in a deadly, live-or-die casino. I imagined Americans walking around with bottles of whisky. The writing on the bottles read: Scotch Johnny Walker, born 1840 and still walking strong.

I took a deep breath and whispered, "Oh no, no-o-o-o-o."

I turned to face the wall. "Is America really where I want to take my children?"

Then I thought about the Sudan Peoples Liberation Army/Movement (SPLA/M), a monopoly of one man. As a part of its modernizing socialist ideology, SPLA/M set out to transform social relations in southern Sudan by force. More controversially, the SPLA/M leadership took a strong stand against African traditional systems. In liberation army controlled areas, communal villages were destroyed. The village people then had no belongings and were forced to rely on relief food. Farming or cultivating food was not possible due to the presence of the liberation army. Because of the resulting instability and insecurity, many people left their villages and moved to neighboring countries.

The Commander-in-Chief of the SPLA/M appointed village secretaries to replace the village elders, but all were from his ethnic group, the Dinka. In some places, a younger brother or cousin of the old leader would be made SPLA/M secretary, so that he carried some traditional authority as well. More often, traditional leaders were simply displaced. The SPLA/M bypassed the traditional courts and created their own local magistrate courts, which were not sensitive to the ethnic diversity in southern Sudan. They labeled traditional healers as witch doctors, and dismissed the traditional clan leaders. Young men loyal to the SPLA/M leadership were appointed to lead villages and displaced camps. This new system created confusion in the villages.

Traditional families were torn apart, as women were coveted by SPLA/M commanders. A woman's appearance could endanger her husband's life. It was not uncommon for husbands to be killed so their wives could be married to senior commanders who supported the SPLA/M leadership. Polygamy among the leadership was widespread, as all the commanders and SPLA/M authorities eagerly accumulated wealth and married as many wives as they liked. Some commanders had fifteen to twenty wives or even more.

Although women were encouraged to join the liberation movement, the majority who did ended up as wives of army officers. The entire women's army unit disintegrated in just three years; not a single female soldier was left in the army. The wife of the Chairman and Commander-in-Chief of the SPLA/M was the leader of the women's army unit. She had the power to influence the killing of anyone she thought was a threat to her husband's leadership. She was responsible for the death of many highly educated southern Sudanese.

Women told me that she formed a group of women to spy on commanders. These spies were unmarried women who used their sexual availability to gather information. This shows the underhandedness in the leadership of the movement, because sex outside of marriage and prostitution are not acceptable among the Nilotic people.

The SPLA/M made overt attacks on churches, local people, and educated southern Sudanese of non-Dinka origin. People who ran businesses and former government officials were not allowed to join the liberation movement. Neither were they allowed to participate in the affairs of their community, because the SPLA/M considered them to be enemies of the movement.

Because of these abuses, many southern Sudanese people fled to the northern part of the country and settled in large shantytowns around the cities. I saw another Cambodia taking shape in the jungles and Savannah of Sudan, with a tyrant like Pol Pot in command.

To achieve the liberation of Sudan, the SPLA/M took children away from their families to join the liberation movement. Some of these boys were as young as the age of seven. They were taught a single ideology that was based in radical Marxism. I knew that my older son Duany, now eight years old, was a potential candidate for being drafted as a child soldier.

My heart started pounding and I jumped out of bed and ran to the children's room. I stood in the darkness, staring at my two little boys, who might not have the chance to grow up if Wal and I failed to make the right decision. I bit my lower lip and said, "How innocent; I must protect these children." Tears rolled down my cheeks. Strangely, I found some comfort in their warmth.

It was almost morning. I crossed restlessly to the window and pushed back the long fluffy blue curtains. From this window I could see in the distance a swirl of lights moving toward *Suk Malikia,* the central market of Juba. I saw people running as fast as their legs could take them across the football (soccer) field, away from the market and into the residential areas of *Haya Ni-miri Thalatha.* Then, outside my house, I heard the murmuring of a group of women carrying baskets on their heads, walking very fast away from the site. I called out and asked them what was going on in the market. They all yelled at the same time, *"Shakila, shakila!* Fight, fight!" It was a fight between Mudari and Dinka Bor tribesmen. That day the police ordered people to stay in their homes, warning them that they must not come out. Over the radio, we heard reports that two people were killed, and fifteen people injured in the market fight.

Terrible things began happening. There was ethnic fighting in the streets, the markets were shut down, and the schools were closed. Many people left the city. Juba was becoming a ruin in the forested hills of Africa. At its best, Juba had been a city inhabited by 60,000 to 70,000 people, including government officials, royal merchants, and countless poor people.

Wal and I had to make a quick decision. Our children were too young to be taken into the bush.

Exodus to Bloomington

We moved north to Khartoum, so our children could attend school. We spent six months in Khartoum, but living conditions there became very hard. Our employment had been in the South so neither of us had income in Khartoum. Life in Juba had been simple. We had our own farm where we kept milk cows. In Khartoum, we had to buy everything. Even the milk which we used to get from our own cows had to be purchased from Arab nomads everyday.

Wal returned to Juba to find somebody to rent our house; this was the only source of income we had. While he was there, Wal spoke to his friend Robert McCanlis, who was Director of the United States Agency for International Development (USAID) in Juba. Mr. McCanlis had arranged a scholarship opportunity with a university in the United States. Wal applied and quickly was admitted for advanced studies at Indiana University at Bloomington. My geography classes in school had not mentioned this place. In Sudan, students study America to learn of its industrial and agricultural advancement. I knew nothing of Indiana.

Wal left for the United States on September 12, 1984. I followed later with the children. Wal was not permitted to travel with his family. If we had left together, it would have raised concerns that he was leaving the country to join the rebel movement. We would have been stopped.

After a week I began the process of getting our traveling documents, which I finally secured with great difficulty. I owe a debt of gratitude to this doctor. He testified on my behalf to the national security forces that I needed special medical care in London. Because he was a Northerner, my doctor's recommendation was acceptable to the gatekeepers at national security. Immigration gave us a three-month exit visa for London.

With nothing but what we carried in a few suitcases, my four young children, the one in my womb, and I started our journey to an unknown land to a new life. We also carried hope—in the United States of America our children could attend school. But it was hard to leave our relatives. Our hearts remained in the Sudan.

The children and I left Khartoum at 10:00 p.m. There were many people at the airport that day. Some had come to pick up their loved ones. Some came to have a good time watching the huge "heaven birds" ascending and descending at intervals. We, and others who were flying that night, busied ourselves with our luggage. I was thinking of my mother and many other relatives who we were leaving behind. I wondered what I could expect in America. Finally our luggage was inspected and our passports stamped. We passed through the security gate for final inspection and were then confined to a small room to wait for our final call to board the aircraft. I began to worry that the security people might try to prevent us from traveling abroad. The children went to the window to watch the airplanes while I sat, feeling as if I was in an isolation booth watching the world go by. I heard a voice announce over the intercom that it was time to board the airplane to London.

We were in the air within a half an hour. The roar of the airplane engines passing over the River Nile disturbed every living creature along the river. I imagined animals grazing in the darkness by the river. The hippopotamus, crocodiles and others with their young would panic and rush back into the water. Early the next morning, as our plane circled London, we had a birds-eye view of the home of kings and queens. I was happy that we had made it out of Khartoum together. My brother, Dr. Barnaba Marial, picked us up at the airport.

"We want to see New York," said Nyagon my oldest daughter.

The younger children kept asking, "Where is that New York, Mom?"

"It is coming," I would reply.

The endless journey made them tired, so they dozed off to sleep.

We had visited London a number of times for holidays. They had seen the London Bridge, the River Thames, and monuments telling the history of the people of Great Britain. They knew how the British invaded nations like swarms of hornets in search of wealth and a warmer climate; how they sharpened their swords and spilled much blood everywhere in the world to create wealth for the British Kingdom. My children had enough of these stories, and did not want to hear any more. They were eager to go to the United States, to see New York, and the gigantic Green Lady of Liberty.

I did not want to stay in London for a week or two either. But being eight months pregnant, I did not think I could fly another eight to ten hours. Thank God the baby decided to come early. Maybe he wanted to have British nationality. Our fifth child was born in London. I named him Bil, after my father. We stayed with my brother another three weeks to allow time for me to recover and the baby to grow strong.

We left London at 6:00 p.m. one evening and followed the sun that never set. It was 3:00 p.m., New York time, when I saw the fasten seatbelt sign light up and heard the captain say, "We are landing in New York." The captain circled the city, waiting for permission to land. I saw huge airplanes passing in the sky. I closed my eyes, paralyzed with fear. I held my hands together and prayed, "Oh God, do not let us crash." The children, sensing no danger, joyfully watched as the airplanes circled. We landed safely at John F. Kennedy (JFK) International Airport. I said my last prayer: "Thank you, God, for the safe landing. Amen."

We were the first to leave the plane. Although they were having fun, the children did not know of what to make of New York. We followed a zigzagging line through immigration to have our passports inspected.

Suddenly my young son Kueth saw a security dog coming towards him. He broke into a wild run towards me, screaming, "*Kalba! Kalba!*" This is an Arabic word for female dog.

"It is okay little guy," said a policeman, pulling the dog away from us.

Kueth has always been afraid of dogs and I don't blame him. He was only five years old. This dog was as big as a calf. It's wide mouth, long red tongue, and sharp teeth seemed larger than Kueth's head.

We received no VIP treatment in New York City, as we had been offered on past trips to London on diplomatic passports. Here there was no one to meet us, no one to help with our luggage, and no car waiting to take us to a hotel. We were on our own.

As we waited in line at immigration, the children's heads moved left and right, taking in the sights. We saw women walk by, swinging their hips and sporting short skirts with a back slit which offered a view of their thighs. The rapping of their high-heeled footsteps sounded like a handy man hammering nails. These women had decorated themselves with heavy makeup, long dark eyelashes, bright lipstick, and long artificial nails. They moved unconsciously, curling their mouths around chewing gum and smacking it loudly. The smacking sound drew the attention of everybody passing by. These women reminded me of *Nissa el weedi*, the medicine-women of Khartoum who decorated themselves with bright colorful beads to attract patrons. The medicine women are experts in reading someone's future.

We saw men with harsh good looks, wrapped in belted trench coats. They looked like models. Their bodies radiated cologne, which stung our nostrils as they passed by.

People of all ages, young and old, intent on their business walked briskly by us. The airport was a crazy world for me, but my children were very excited and happy. "So this is New York, a busy, busy, place where nothing could cause a head of a New Yorker to turn," I said to myself.

Finally we reached the immigration desk. Behind the desk sat a large man, well over six feet tall, weighing about two hundred pounds, and wearing a crisp shirt. His appearance was not friendly; he did not smile and he made no eye contact. He looked like Mr. No-Nonsense. A man with a job to do. He presented to me the stereotypic image of the Western World: "Time is money."

I handed him our documents.

"Where are you going?" he asked while turning pages in the passport. He evidently did not know where to look, because the passport was written in Arabic, which is written from right to left. He rolled his eyes and said, "Where does it start?" I watched as he struggled to find the page.

I pointed to the right side of the passport. He turned it over and sharply asked me, "Where are you going?"

"Bloom-aa-aa, Bloom-ing-ton," I answered.

I had difficulty hearing the man. He had a deep voice and my ears were affected by the pressure change on the long flight. He frowned and repeated my words very quickly. I understood English, but I was not used to American accents; all I heard was the "Bl" at the beginning and the "tn" at the end at the end. The rest of the sounds disappeared in his mouth and came out through his nose.

"Bloomington!" he said loudly. "There are many Bloomingtons in the United States. You have to know the state."

"Indiaaa—," I started.

Before I could finish, he said, "Indiana."

He then asked me many questions in a very short time, confusing me. He spoke very fast and had no time to waste. I did not understand all of the questions, but to make things easier I nodded and said, "Yes." Finally he looked at me intently. I saw through his glasses his big, wide open bug-eyes.

"Do you understand what I am saying?"

"Yes," I said and winked, trying to be smart. But to tell the truth, I had never felt so stupid in my life. I understood very little of what he was saying. His mouth moved like a robot that had been programmed to only ask questions. The only thing I could compare this man with was an answering machine that talked and talked without stopping.

In Sudan, people take their time and speak slowly when addressing people they do not know. It is considered rude to speak fast. This immigration officer did not seem to be concerned at all whether or not we understood English. Dealing with this African mother in her late twenties and five children must have been a nightmare for him. He cleared our documents and got us out of his way. I suspected that in the mind of this New Yorker, we were an African tribe.

Now the Duanys were ready to face the New World. But we were momentarily lost in the airport among the flow of New Yorkers marching like ants in a busy colony. The mass movement of people made me think that New York was being evacuated. I became frightened, and I kept my eyes on my children so I would not lose them.

I had a vision of mothers keeping their eyes on their children on the day the cattle camp was moved. There is nothing like the drama in a new Nilotic cattle camp, with the crying of the little children who have lost their mothers, and the calling of the mothers, running around like mother warthogs, searching for their children. All the while the men were busy building *rakuba*, (wigwams or rough huts) for the family, to protect them at night from wild dogs and hyenas. The memory of cattle bells in the Savannah plains overwhelmed me, and brought back the thought of a time gone forever.

Beyond the tall third-floor windows in the airport concourse we saw the New York City sky scrapers, a jungle of concrete, which in the darkening October evening, was blossoming into glitter and sparkle. In the concourse below, the crowd had begun to thin. Outside a street light changed and the headlights of the cars were poked on through the fall of thin, slanting rain. Across the terminal we saw a steady flow of pedestrians dragging luggage, some leaving and some arriving at the airport. We saw businessmen and women going over their assignments in corner bistros, grabbing a bite to eat before catching their flights.

I led the children through the airport to the domestic flight area, where we were to make our connection to Indianapolis, Indiana. While waiting there, we sat near a young, sophisticated-looking couple. The man paid more attention to his hand on the woman's leg than he did to her conversation. The lady ignored his overtures, but focused on sucking the mint in her mouth. I was uncomfortable with their behavior, so I decided to move to another area to keep my children away from them. It was my first encounter with American freedom. In Sudan, couples could never behave that way in a public place. If it ever happened, the offenders would be severely punished. The punishment is thirty lashes and three months imprisonment. People can do whatever they like in their houses, but not in public. I thought that this kind of permissive freedom was responsible for the many scenes of open lovemaking I had seen on American television programs.

At 9:00 p.m., we arrived in Indianapolis. Wal and a friend had come to the airport to pick us up. It took an hour to drive to our final destination. Bloomington, Indiana became the second home for the Duany family. We now have lived more than eighteen years in this humble city.

Our first home was Tulip Tree Apartment #218, in an Indiana University student housing building eleven stories tall and shaped like a half circle. As it is the only housing facility on campus that can accommodate large families, Tulip Tree is well known for its many young, large families who live there. It has been nicknamed the Fertility Center. The playground is always full of young children.

On our first night in Bloomington, I did not sleep well because I was afraid that fire would break out in the building. Before coming to the United States, I had seen pictures on international television news showing building after building burning to ashes in the United States. I kept checking the walls to make sure that they were made of concrete or bricks, and not wood. Despite my fears, I was celebrating our arrival very heartily. "Now there will be stability to our family," I thought.

We spent a week recovering from jet lag. During the day we slept and then we stayed up all night watching television which never went off the air. The first time I went grocery shopping I was amazed to see the kinds of food products one could buy: meat, fruits, vegetables, canned foods. Even the animal pets had their own food section.

As October gave way to November, and then to December, the weather changed from warm Fall to Arctic Winter. It seemed Arctic to us. This was the first time we had experienced winter weather. We bought heavy clothes. I felt awkward and clumsy in my first winter coat. It made me feel fat.

One morning I looked out the window of our apartment and saw white ash dropping from heaven. At first I thought there was something wrong with our building, so I watched very carefully, trying to figure out what it was. The strange stuff continued to come down all over the place, as if from a volcanic eruption or a dust storm of the Sahara Desert. Then I realized it was snow. I rushed to the children's rooms and told them that snow was falling. They jumped out of their beds and scrambled to the door, without their shoes, to see the first snow of the winter of 1984.

Outside, we found some children already playing with snowballs. My children joined the game, but quickly became too cold because they were not dressed properly. We went back inside to put on our winter clothes. This time we were smart. We put on boots, gloves, and coats, but it was still too cold for us to stay outside for long. I could see steam coming out of peoples' mouths. I remember that day very well; it was a Saturday, and the children spent the whole day coming in and going out into the cold ash from heaven.

In Bloomington, I saw people of all types different nationalities. Most of them were students attending Indiana University. There were many Africans, from the tall ebony Senegalese of the Mandingo nation to short brown-skinned Kung from the Kalahari Desert. Some of the international students had families, and their children attended the school my children would attend. I was happy to be in a place were my children would meet people of other nationalities.

I stayed home for three months to care for Bil, my baby, but I was lonely. I had no friends and no family nearby. I decided to enroll in the School of Education at Indiana University to finish my Bachelor's degree, which I had not been able to finish after the University of Juba had closed. The Presbyterian Church (USA) sponsored me to finish my degree, and that is how I became a student again in January 1985.

The classes at Indiana University were very different from those I had taken at the universities in Sudan. First of all, my classmates were people of all different ages. In Sudan, older students were enrolled in separate programs known as Adult Education. In my apartment building, there were several African and

Black American families, but to my surprise, there were no Black American students in my classes; I wondered why.

I later learned that few black Americans attend college, and that those who do generally do not select schools in small Midwestern towns like Bloomington. During my first year in Indiana I read much Black American literature. The first was *Black Boy* by Richard Wright. Wright wrote about his experience growing up in a racist world created by White European Americans. This book helped me understand the history of race relations in America. It also helped me to adjust to my New World.

Nevertheless, I enjoyed my first classes because the professors were so knowledgeable in their subjects. To me, the classes in this American university were easy because of the availability of learning materials. We were assigned a lot of reading material for each class. Professors assigned 250-300 pages per week plus a book review. I enjoyed the challenge, because I had my own books. In Sudan, we students read only 60 to 100 pages per week because of the lack of study materials. However, it was a bit of a shock when I first discovered that in each class I attended the professors were assigning hundreds of pages of reading. I wondered whether or not these professors knew what they were doing. I asked one of my classmates, "Do these professors know that we are not taking only one class?"

"They only care about their own subjects," she said. "You just have to do the work and keep up."

After that day I never complained. I did my best to complete my schoolwork, never stopping until March 1996, the day I defended my dissertation.

I also was surprised by the cultural differences between American and Sudanese students. In Sudan, students respect their teachers. Students do not sit with their legs on chairs, drinking coffee or tea, or even eating in the classroom while the professor is lecturing. I was shocked to see American students doing these things in class and thought that they were very rude. When I saw women wearing shorts in front of a male professor, it made me very uncomfortable. And I felt ashamed if the male professors looked at me too directly. I would look away, avoiding eye contact with male professors.

Indiana University is many times larger than the University of Khartoum, the major institution of higher learning in Sudan. There were over one hundred students in one of my classes. Technology has made the American institution more efficient, but sometimes the computer punch cards seemed to be more important than the human beings they represented. The first time I registered for classes, I felt that I was nothing but a number. In one of my undergraduate classes, the professor asked us students to put their student ID numbers on our papers instead of our names. I asked the professor why we could not use our names. He said, "It is more objective; I won't know who is who until I total up the final grades."

Because my first semester began in January, I had to walk long distances back and forth across the campus in very cold weather to attend my classes. One day, it snowed. I did not know how to walk on the snow. I walked like a baby who was learning to walk. It was so slippery that I lost my footing and fell hard on the ground. I looked around to see if someone would come to my aid, but no one came. I sat there for a few minutes, pulling myself together. I got up and continued to walk to my class. My clothes were dirty, but there was no time to go home and change. Thank God I did not break a bone, but I had a big cut on my left knee. No one in class seemed to notice my appearance; not a single soul asked me what had happened to my knee. I walked home very disappointed. I thought people did not care.

"*Waa!*" (It's a Nuer expression of surprise.) "What happened?" asked Wal, who noticed the cut the minute I stepped into the apartment.

"I fell," It was a big cut, about two inches long. By that time, I no longer felt pain because I was so cold from walking. Later, the scar on my left knee became my American birthmark, an African woman's first serious encounter with snow.

I quickly discovered that American institutions of higher learning are market-oriented. They function like a profit-making business. All services are based on their dollar value. I have to be honest whenever anyone asks me what I think of the universities in America. I tell them the bad thing is that financially, it is difficult to get an American education. The good thing, however, is that the door to higher education is open to anyone who really wants to go to college. In Sudan, higher education is supported by taxes, so students are not responsible for paying the cost. But many students compete for the limited spaces in the university. The doors open to very few.

My interest in social issues had formed as I became a young adult during the late 1960s. By the 1980s, during my undergraduate work, I had come face to face with realities of this body of knowledge. I delved into social issues, especially those of human rights, race, and gender. I studied apartheid in South Africa, racism in America, and atrocities in Nazi

Germany. I read books about real peoples and their suffering. I learned about Japanese imperialism, the atomic bombing of Hiroshima, and injustice all over the world. I wanted to learn everything. My undergraduate studies began my renaissance.

My thoughts broadened in terms of adding wisdom to my nature, clarity to my vision, and glamour to my person. I was born, grew up, and attended school in southern Sudan, where life is influenced by Islamic culture because of the historical domination of northern governments. Islam is the order of the day, and its tradition ordains women's lives, making them second class citizens. Elementary education may not be available to these women, and if it is, the opportunity is not valued. For these women, higher education is impossible. Some of the young women who attended school with me in Sudan were persuaded to cut their schooling so they could marry or earn money to support their families.

Some of the young women who dropped out of school found it difficult to fit back into village life. These young women became products of the new sex industry supported by the tourist trade. Rich Arabs visiting from the Middle East were attracted to their black bodies and baby-faces. Middle Eastern black gold (oil) provided them with wealth and opportunity to wander around Africa. These Arab men searched for young African women with large breasts, slender bellies, big bones, and solid bodies. The young women hung out in the big hotels, hoping to be picked up by some rich older man. These men were known on the street as Sugar Daddies. The young women needed money and the Sugar Daddies needed someone to hold them tight with the assurance that their wives back home would never find out.

Because I had seen these extremes in Sudan, I understood the difficulties that women face in their lives because of the lack of education and social status. I strongly believed that the women's movement needed women leaders who understood these difficulties. I felt that there was a need for women in developing countries to learn to be more than just housewives. They needed education so that they could keep up with modern trends. Yes, there were problems, but I was certain there were solutions.

My graduate work caused me to search, not for theory, but for action. I felt alienated in my field because most of the writing about women in developing nations reflects a Western cultural bias. One of my greatest frustrations is with literature labeled "The Third World Woman," "Women in Development," or "Empowering Women." Gender scholars have a tendency to treat women in developing countries as if they are a homogeneous group. They too readily assume that all women share a common heritage and common experience. Gender scholars also pay little attention to the effects of different economic ways of life, political systems, cultures, and social organizations within and among geographical regions. My understanding of gender issues went beyond the cliches of the women's studies debates and the representation of women as a monolithic group.

My heart has always directed my interest in focusing on women's experiences. My purpose in investigating social issues was to be able to understand and find factors that shape social structure and the way these structures affect people in what might be called a "real" situation. As a scholar, I was eager for hands-on, face-to-face inquiry that would permit me to

157

comprehend people's stories and their experiences in this deeper context.

The Challenge of Migration

Early one morning during my first semester at Indiana University in January 1985, I stood outside a classroom and watched the sun peeking through the clouds. It was my habit to rate the sunrise on a scale from 0 to 10 every morning of that first Bloomington winter. Dark clouds skimmed the sky, and I wished for a little sun to warm me up. The gray clouds spit white heaven ashes (snow) at me. It still did not seem natural. On the ground and on the road the heaven-ash had piled inch deep. I could not see well because the snow in the air was too thick. After I had my first bad fall, I was afraid to walk on snow. I had the option of either walking or riding the bus. I rode the bus that day.

As the bus steered along the snowy road, I began to dream. I have a fantasy of a land of milk and honey, of love and peace, freedom and happiness, and of good weather and a good life. For many new immigrants to America, there is this unconscious longing for paradise—the image of a happy new life where all needs are fulfilled. We are all susceptible to projecting these grand fantasies of Eden onto an unfamiliar culture or place. We are equally susceptible to the feelings of despair that arise from a sense of paradise lost or never fully gained. In America, I wanted to find what I had lost. I wanted to find something that I never fully had—the devotion to a culture, the glory of success, and the freedom from pain and conflict—because of the cultural, political, and religious conflict in my homeland.

Most people have fantasies and hopes of finding a better life somewhere else. The initial stage of immigration can be marked by excitement: the dream has been fulfilled, the fantasy has come true, the obstacles have been surmounted. However, like the beginning of a love affair, this stage usually does not last very long. Idealization cannot hold, so the reality brings disillusionment. At the same time, new conflicts are experienced. For people escaping oppressive political regimes, as my family did, the fantasy may be intertwined with the desire to free ourselves from violence. For example, some immigrants from Africa and Eastern Europe grew up in totalitarian regimes, and often saw the industrialized Western nations as the polar opposites of the political systems in their own home countries. Before I came to America, I saw the industrialized nations as dreamlike worlds of freedom and unlimited possibilities. This picture was reinforced by the international media, which often represents the world as split into the "good" industrialized nations and the "bad" underdeveloped (Third World) nations. There are no shades of gray in this developed/underdeveloped view of the world today.

Many of my friends in Sudan who have never visited an industrialized nation criticize their own political system. They view their own world as all bad and the industrialized world as all good. For them, realistic information about the outside world is scarce and travel to the industrialized nations is limited. The media further reinforces their idealization of the industrialized world.

I know from conversations with recent southern Sudanese immigrants to the United States, people having had no previous experience living or traveling abroad, that fantastic expectations of life in America are common. These immigrants expected to acquire everything magically upon their arrival in the States. They came with attitudes formed by the media, including the expectation that they could depend upon the American welfare system for support.

Complicating their lack of cultural knowledge was their fearful tendency to see the New World as unfriendly. This is because the Sudanese immigrants, coming from a totalitarian environment, harbored an unconscious fear of punishment by authority, coupled with a hidden resentment toward it. Therefore, these immigrants often cannot bring themselves to trust new ways of resolving conflicts. As a result, they are resistant to resolving any genuine differences of opinion through dialogue or compromise, have a hard time resolving their own personal conflicts, and have become isolated from the cultural mainstream.

Such attitudes and characteristics tend to develop when people grow up in a system where free expression is impossible or dangerous, where initiative is severely punished, and where authoritarian rule prevails. These attitudes become deeply entrenched and are very slow to change. Many of these immigrants arrive unprepared to face realistic challenges. It took me months to adjust and to accept my new challenges. But by watching and doing, I learned new ways of resolving the day-to-day problems I encountered in my new environment.

Many refugees come to America from non-English speaking nations. They never thought of leaving their own homelands or learning the English language. They are totally unprepared for living abroad. Their past experiences are limited; and they often focus on what they had to leave behind rather than on what they want to build. They struggle with enormous obstacles. For example, I saw some of my African colleagues who were good parents, but could not hold on to their families in America. They divorced and struggled as single parents.

I was in search of my imagined Paradise Lost. In my youth and adolescence, my fantasy of going abroad to study was a way of keeping hope alive in the most difficult times of oppression and personal crises. This fantasy was based on my desire for new opportunities. By escaping abroad, I hoped to find a way of being whole and finding love, happiness, and freedom. This youthful fantasy did not last very long for me. Now as an adult, I was faced with the reality. I found myself torn apart: one part of me searching for a way to return home, and the other part of me searching for new ways of life. In the New World I wished to regain what I had lost, to find those parts of me that now were distant.

Feelings of uncertainty make emigration a stressful process. One leaves behind beloved people and a familiar culture. Comfortable patterns of living and relationships with people are disrupted. In leaving Sudan I lost the sense of belonging, epitomized by being intuitively understood in one's native language and culture. I lost the subjective feeling of safety and connectedness. These multiple and profound losses are burdens I carried while striving to adapt to a new language and culture. The effort to adapt is accompanied by mourning for the abandoned life. Gradually, over a period of some years, I worked through the emotions evoked by painful losses in order to adapt successfully. For many immigrants, this lengthy process begins after an initial period of culture shock. As a new immigrant, I found myself among strangers in an unfamiliar environment. My usual ways of relating to people were no longer appropriate or understandable. The impact of this alien culture was overwhelming; my attempt to deal with feelings of anxiety and confusion profoundly tested the overall adequacy of my personality. A sense of discontinuity severely threatened my identity. The solution to the problem is to look for new options and create a new identity. People who cling to their original cultural ways have problems adjusting.

During my first months in the United States, I did not understand that the phrase "how are you?" is a greeting that is often answered superficially. When asked this question by a colleague, I was inclined to describe at length the feelings of depression and the difficulties I was experiencing in my new environment. Once, as I was telling an American friend "how I was," I noticed that she had a stunned expression and remained silent while I disclosed my pain. She cut the conversation short and apologized to me because, as she said, she was late for class. Later I understood that she was at a loss as to how to respond to my outpouring. In my native Nilotic culture, it is common for people to share their troubles with their friends, and not to pretend that everything is okay. It is considered natural to express one's feelings and to complain about problems to friends and family members. This is simply part of the natural discourse between people in my culture. Americans, I discovered, are different.

Maybe one reason Americans display a sunny, optimistic, strong image is because of the value they place on success and achievement. The dark side of life is often denied, experienced only privately, or explored in psychotherapy. In my opinion, superficiality is an underlying reason for many of the problems faced by young people in industrialized societies. Social issues that need to be discussed with young people are hidden until a crisis erupts. During my first years in the United States, I did not recognize this social practice of making things look better than they are. I struggled with the need to air my problems because, like almost everyone else, I sometimes needed somebody to talk to. I wanted to be happy and achieve success in this new life, but I did not want to struggle alone. I was fortunate in Bloomington to be associated with a church where I found some friends with whom I could share my feelings openly.

Making Friends Brings Joy

I cannot close this chapter without describing what happened in my life after making new friends. For my emotional and mental well being, it was of the utmost importance that I learn the value of building respect and trust for others by crossing cultural and racial lines to make friends. My fear of trust may seem strange, but remember that I had come from a world of treachery, where trusting the wrong person could cost both Wal and me our lives.

In my strange New World, I was confronted with many things in too large a dose to swallow at once. Trust, especially, was something I had to learn to accept one step at a time. I began that journey on a Saturday in 1985, when my oldest son Duany asked me to watch him play basketball at the local Boys Club. It was the first basketball game I had ever attended. At the game, I met a woman who later became like a sister to me. Nancy Ireland had three children, Joshua, Micah and Isaiah. She was pregnant with their fourth child, Kali. The friendship of Nancy and her husband Kelly made my family and me feel at home in Bloomington.

My encounter with Nancy's heartfelt trust and friendship did so much to show me how I could fit in to this culture, where lineage and clan affiliation counted for so little. I saw that nothing draws people to each other as effectively as a heart filled with enthusiastic love and friendship. The ability to trust emerged in my life like a glorious spring morning. I learned that trust is made up of a multitude of small things and that there is no way to measure the value of true friendship. Through the friendship of one woman, who I met at a basketball game, my fearful outlook began to change into one of exquisite happiness and joy. The lessons of friendship, trust, and respect that I learned from Nancy are what have made my years in America so great.

Years later, when I taught in the Monroe County Community School Corporation (MCCSC), these lessons were invaluable. Some of the children I met at the school were fearful and trusted no one.

In September 1995, I met a student who was in the fifth grade in one of the county schools. He was a good boy, but fear had taken over his life. He had no friends and the other children made fun of him. His parents were in their mid thirties, recently divorced, and having a hard time understanding each other. Their son became the link of their only communication. He lived with his mother and visited his father on weekends. He could not sit still during lessons; he could be disruptive and even violent. He had developed his own ways of controlling his environment.

As his teacher, I had to find ways to resolve the problem he was creating in the classroom. I thought of the courage of Daisy Bates. I had read about the life of Daisy Bates, the heroic teacher who crossed the line to fight for integration in Little Rock, Arkansas, in the 1950's. Daisy faced bigger problems then than I now had with this boy. She eventually took on 11,000 soldiers to assure nine black children their constitutional rights. If Daisy could help millions of American people to improve human relations by doing what was right, then I could do something to help this boy and his classmates get along.

One day, the boy became very angry in the classroom. Nothing went right for him that day. He threw his books and his lunch box across the room. I asked him to sit still, but he would not. I started counting, "Five. Four. Three. Two. One…one and a half. Zero. Okay, you either sit quietly with the class or you go and sit by yourself."

"I will sit by myself," he said.

I was happy he decided to sit alone, because he had been so difficult that morning he almost brought tears to my eyes. I felt helpless, but I had to act quickly to find a way to engage him and give him something to do so that I could return my attention to the other children. I asked him if he could write a story about his family. That suggestion hit the nail on the head. He started writing and later handed me the following story:

Yesterday it was a day to go back to my Dad so I went and hid in the closet. My Mom told me that we have to eat supper before it is time to go back to my Dad.

She said to me, "Your Jell-O is going to melt before you even get to see it jiggle. It's lime green with orange carrot shreds for hair. Maybe you just need a hug, is that it? I haven't had a good hug today, either. I am crawling in there with a big He Man hug today here I come."

She opened the door, got me out and kissed me.

She said, "Okay! I am your mommy. It does not matter where I live. I will always be your mommy."

I told my Mom that I do not want to go to Dad today. "Please, can I have more time with you. I get to see you only one night a week and I miss you a lot."

But she did not listen to me. She only said, "I know you miss me. But I do not hate you. I love you. You are my little boy, remember? Listen, honey, come out and let me hold you. Please."

I came out and she held me that made her feel better but not me. What do you think I can do Mrs. Duany?

Sometimes we (adults) have difficulty knowing how to respond to a situation like this, especially when the child clearly needs someone he or she can trust. This was my big test; I had to be there to meet this child's need. I had to help him find a solution to his problem, but I was at a loss.

"Okay," I said. "Stop being mad at everyone." I smiled but he did not.

"Did I say something?" I asked again. "Tell me. What did I do?"

I placed paper and crayons in front of him.

"I tell you what," I said. "You draw a picture or write me a note, okay?"

He wrote this note:

Dear Mrs. Duany:
I am very, very mad with my parents.
They never allow me to stay in one
place. I hate to be moving every time

166

they want me to. I wish I stayed in one
place. Can you tell my Mom please, that
I hate moving?
Thank you very much.
Yours,

He gave me the note and returned to his desk. I
read his note and it broke my heart. I thought there
must be thousands of school children in American
classrooms who are like this boy, crying for help. I
wanted to help him. He had become part of my life.

I had a conference with the boy's parents to
discuss the note he wrote. The parents agreed to let
him stay with his mother during the school season and
to live with his father during the holidays. Our
conference worked things out very well. The boy
settled down and became a good student. He no longer
created a problem in the classroom.

As a teacher, I learned to listen. I discovered
that behind troubling behavior was a troubled child's
need to speak and to be heard. My student learned to
confide in someone he could trust. He discovered that
even though his parents were having difficulties, they
were willing to adapt to meet his needs. I will never
forget friends like this student, who taught me more
about listening, trusting, and reaching out to others.

When we prove that we are trustworthy, when
people see in us the treasure of respect and trust, they
are attracted to seek the same for themselves. We are a
community. We are all part of each other, and our
individual behavior, whether good or evil, affects the
whole community.

Nok, Nyagon,
Bil, Kueth, and Duany

Chapter VI

Hoosier Madness

We landed in basketball country: Bloomington, Indiana, the village of Bobby Knight. Soon my eyes were on the basketball. My children's hands were on the basketball. Together, we learned the Hoosier tradition.

My Eyes on the Basketball

Where I grew up children played games outside. My brothers and their friends energetically kicked about a homemade football (soccer ball) of plastic and rags on a grassy, open ground football court.

After we came to Indiana we soon learned about a new game. On winter days, the people of Indiana float through memories of basketball games. I discovered a basketball madness swirling about like the cold winter air, exciting the skin and agitating people so that they cannot sit still. People are drawn to the gymnasium like ants to the colony, marching in line to their work routine.

I vividly remember the evening when I first attended a boys' high school basketball game gymnasium at Bloomington North High School. It was cold, early February. Entering the gym, I heard the echo of dribbling basketballs, the shouts of cheerleaders, and the expectant clamor of the fans. The young athletes, with their heads held high, handled themselves proudly in their uniforms on the court.

Wal, the children, and I found seats in the lower part of the gym, close to the players and the action. My attention was drawn to a little boy sitting near me and eating popcorn.

"Do you like popcorn?" I asked.

"Yes," was the reply.

"You do? Me too. I know all little boys like popcorn on a night like this!" I said.

He jumped up and ran to his mother, who was sitting right behind us. I guess I was interfering with his concentration on the game. He seemed not to miss any move on the court. I remembered this boy became he later became one of my fifth grade students. He was the most polite, hard working student I ever came across during my teaching in Bloomington. Doak Henry later played on the same basketball team with my youngest son Bil. I came to know Doak's family, and to this day he and Bil are very good friends.

After Duany introduced his brothers and sisters to basketball, the Duany family spent most of our winter evenings in high school basketball gymnasiums. It became the common place where we all met after finishing our daily activities at work and school.

During the off-season, Duany spent most of his time with good friend Joshua McAfee at the Boys Club gymnasium. After finishing their homework, the boys would play basketball for hours. They never seemed to tire of if. Besides basketball, our children were involved in many different sports. Wal and I found ourselves spending hours in the car, taking the children in different directions—Nyagon to a track meet, Nok to soccer practice, Kueth to play a baseball game, Bil to be picked up at the Boys Club.

My typical week began on Sunday morning, with the challenge of getting five kids and one husband ready for the drive to church. Six-month old Bil woke me at 5:00 a.m., making a *waa, waa, waa* sound. Unfortunately, this was not enough to wake the rest of the family. I was a Mommy-Monster, shaking little boys who did not want to get up. I was on a serious schedule, skidding back into my room to answer Wal's morning questions.

"Julia, have you seen my blue shirt? Where are my black socks?"

"That shirt is hanging in the closet," I said. "And the socks are in the lower drawer." And away I went. I had no time to pull out the shirt or to find the black socks.

After church services, things calmed down. Our day ended with a late Sunday dinner and getting the children into bed. Once the children were settled, I had time for a ten-minute shower and to brush my teeth. The apartment was peaceful, and I had the luxury of two to three quiet hours to read my class work for Monday.

Mondays and Wednesdays I had to be at my Comparative Education class at 10:00 a.m. I had English Writing class three times a week at noon. On Thursday evening, I had an Anthropology class.

In the mornings I felt like a robot. I allotted the final fifteen minutes every morning before I left the apartment to drink my hot tea, help my husband find things, send the children to the school bus, and take the baby to the baby-sitter. In the bathroom there could be five loads of laundry to wash, the overflowing baskets squatting sadly as if they were not wanted. As I hurried about the apartment, I would try not to look at those baskets.

Finally the clock, that relentless machine hanging on the wall, ticked away, told me it was time to go. The last thing I saw as I closed the door behind me was the morning pile of dishes in the sink. "It's okay," I would nod my head and say. "I will be back to wash you guys."

At noon during the week, I forced down food without much chewing; I could emulsify a turkey sandwich in three minutes, leaving forty-seven minutes to pick up my daughter at kindergarten and take her to a baby-sitter.

Home by 5:00 p.m., I prepared dinner before the kids came home. At 6:00 p.m. I left to pick up my son at basketball practice. Returning, we might find Wal in his jogging suit setting off for some exercise before dinner. Finally we all assembled in the living room to see who needed help with his or her homework. At 9:30 p.m., it was time for a story and bed.

Then I would leap to the computer to work on my term papers. The children usually left it on, so first I had to take a few seconds to exit their games. Writing is part of college life. I struggled all week to write papers such as "The Role of Gender, Education, and Development in Africa," knowing that my words would not convince a Western feminist professor that African women do not necessarily live lives of oppression. I tried my best to explain life in Africa from an African perspective.

At 11:30 p.m., I would go to the kitchen to unwind as I washed the dishes, pots, and pans and put away the leftover food. It took me only fifteen minutes to clean the small kitchen. With plenty of left over food in the refrigerator, I always thought about the many people in the world who were not so lucky as I was. I had seen statistics that said 157 million people, or 3 percent of the world's population, live in countries currently affected by famine or food shortages. Sudan is one of these countries. I often wondered, "How can we stop hunger?" The answer was always the same: only through peace. I tried to comfort my aching soul.

On Saturdays, I would arise from my coma at 5:00 a.m. and race to beat the clock I had a son to get to a basketball game and daughter to take to a track meet. The rush of blood in the body inspires.

On Friday and Saturday nights from 6:00 to 10:30 p.m., I worked part time at Indiana University serving food in one of the dormitory dining halls. This job was to help pay our rent. Standing on my feet for four and a half hours took a toll on my back. By the time I got home, I was not able to bend over to pick up my baby without biting my lower lip. I would give him a kiss and say, "Oh, sweetie, Mommy is here." He would give me a smile, the comforting language of children.

My life in America had become a race, a test of endurance I had to either win or lose. When things fell apart in my homeland, I grasped the baton and began running, stumbling at times, but never quitting and never losing hope. I tried to instill in my children a sense of purpose and self-sufficiency so they could run this race as well. My children conformed to new ways of life better than I dared hope. Yet there are many more miles to run.

In America, I was not sure how I was going to keep my children out of trouble. I saw so many poor role models within the culture: entertainers with serial marriages, pop stars with skimpy clothes and colored hair, comedians with incessant crude stories, and athletes with self-indulgent lifestyles. Where were the people who inspired young people and gave them courage? With so many images in the culture competing for the children's loyalty, Mom and Dad made sure they always knew where the little Duanys were. Wal and I believe that teaching morals starts at home, with both parents making the effort to be there for the children. For us, the effort was a pleasure, because we really enjoyed every moment spent with our children, whether at sport events, school activities, or around the dinner table. After school Wal and I knew that if our children were not playing basketball, they were either in the apartment or at the library doing their schoolwork.

According to the Nilotic culture, a child's life is in the hands of his or her parents. Most of the time, the adults do the talking and the child listens with great expectations. This is a way of telling the little ones, "I care about you." When the adults show what to do, then the child knows what to do when he or she grows up. To me, parenting seems to be a matter of focusing plain energy on life-building.

Though I struggled to complete my education and help support the family, I believed that my children deserved all of my time and attention. I did my best to give it to them, so that they would learn to make the right decisions in life. They observed the way I did things, both in our home and in the outside world. They heard the way I spoke to other people and saw how I chose my friends. I praised them when they imitated me. I made a conscious effort to take the negative images out of my head and emphasize the positive things in life. I taught them what I knew and what I understood about life, so that they could each come to their own understanding. I wanted them to find direction and goals. I wanted each of them to develop their own personality. I wanted the children to take on little challenges as they were able, but I did not want them to become overwhelmed, confused, or shaken in their confidence.

I also learned that sometimes, a parent has to stand back and let the child find his or her own way. This lesson was brought home to me one day as I watched my two little girls, Nyagon and Nok, play with a doll. They were trying to undress the doll, but having trouble with the buttons. They started with the button under the collar. Then they moved to the second button and then the third. I saw their little fingers underneath the shirt and their fingernails scratching at the little pearl buttons. I tried to take the doll so that I could show them what to do, but they pulled her away.

I said, "No!" Then I talked for a minute about the way children ought to behave and about respect. "You have to learn to listen to people," I said.

But they just went right on undressing the doll. They did their own thing and finally unbuttoned the doll's shirt. They learned to undo the buttons on their own, without Mom's help and despite her protests.

"See Mom, we did it," they said, confidently holding up the little shirt.

"I see. Good job, young ladies."

One evening shortly after that incident, I came home from class cold and tired. As soon as I entered the apartment the girls rushed to help me. They pulled off my coat and then began to unbutton my sweater. They had to wiggle their fingers around inside the sweater to get a grip on the big buttons. I was chilled to the bone, and their little hands warmed me.

"Ooh—Mom, you are so cold," they said, and began to rub my back with their warm hands. "You're so cool and smooth," they said.

I did not try to correct the girls this time. I just watched and listened as they put what they had learned from play into practice: helping Mom unbutton her sweater and get warm. I realized anew that my children needed not only my example, but also my trust to guide them through real life learning.

Change of the Tradition

My mother had particular beliefs about the ways in which the future of her children were determined. She believed that a child had to be raised in the Nilotic community. He or she must know about the cattle and how to care for the herds. Time and circumstance have brought radical change in our family life. Our Nilotic traditional way of life has given way to other ways. Our youngest son Bil, who has never been to Africa, knows a lot about cars but very little about cows.

Some of the new ways are better. One is the relationship my children have with their father. In America, Wal was free to interact with our young children. He has become much closer to them than he ever would have in Africa.

Among the Nilotic, the infants and toddlers are rarely in company with their fathers. This is because men spend most of their time away from their homes, either working in the fields and looking after the cattle in the *toich* (flood plain), or talking under the trees with men of their own age about community affairs. Nilotic mothers teach their young children to show respect for their father by not playing roughly or

176

making noise in his presence. The child refrains from physical contact with his or her father and pays attention when Father speaks. The child's gender does not determine the degree of contact between father and child during early childhood. Later on, fathers will spend more time with their sons (and occasionally with their daughters), cooperating in such chores as taking care of the cattle, working in the fields, and teaching them to do the work associated with their life style. Even as an older child spends some time in his or her father's company, usually helping in the work, the distance and reserve in the relationship increases.

Bil, who came to America as an infant, was especially fortunate. The paternal bond he formed with his father developed during infancy. When Bil was an infant and a toddler, Wal held him, talked to him, and played with him just as an American father does. This close interaction made them good friends. When Bil got in trouble with one of his older brothers or sisters, his father would defend him. Now everyone in the house affectionately says Bil is a spoiled child, because his dad helps him all the time.

Nilotic mothers, too, sometimes have limited direct contact with their infants and toddlers, because they must spend most of their time in home management activities. All Nilotic mothers are working mothers, with heavy workloads apart from the care of children. The majority of human contact a young Nilotic child has is from his or her grandparents or from older children. Grandparents assume most of the responsibility for socializing the young children.

Older children have a great deal of responsibility. The girl who looks after a child, *nya mi toot mirom gat*, is usually between the ages of eight and twelve. She is usually an older sibling or close a relative. Childcare is not a problem in the Nilotic society. If a family does not have children old enough to take care of the little ones, they borrow a child from relatives for a period of some years—usually a girl on the mother's side (either a young sister or niece). The family takes care of the borrowed child as their own. She is clothed, fed, and, if she goes to school, she is provided with school fees, a uniform, and other items she may need. If the family abuses the child, they will be denied the right to borrow any other relative's child. The family that borrows a child must continually prove to the relatives that they can be trusted to raise that child.

When my niece Jam was seven years old, my sister gave her to me. Jam was the first child Wal and I had in our home after we married. After Jam came to live with me, never lived in her mother's home again. She saw her parents only when we went to our hometown for holidays. Jam joined me in the United States and continued her studies in higher education at Vincennes University and Iowa State University.

Boys also may be borrowed. Families with no young boys available for the responsibility of *dhol hok*, or herd boy, may borrow a child from relatives. Most often the borrowed boy is one of the husband's nephews. Traditionally, the care of adult cattle is the work of *wud hok*, young men aged fourteen and older. It is a hard business, since it requires defending the herds from raiders or beasts of prey.

In addition to Jam, we raised several of Wal's nephews. They were not herd boys, but while they lived with us we provided for their schooling.

Because pastoral life depends upon every member of the household's labor, both old and young, it is an economic necessity for every household to have children of a certain ages. Not every married couple has its own children in each age category, and this is why the practice of fostering is common. The practice trains the children to be friendly, outgoing, and willing to leave their parents or caretakers in order to accompany relatives. Adults respect an open-minded child.

The Nilotic people believe that children trust only those adults who treat them right. People frequently test a child who is living with a relative by saying, "I am going to visit your mother. Would you like to come with me?" If the child agrees to go, the adults launch an inquiry into the child's living conditions. If a child declines, the relatives he or she lives with receive strong approval. If an adult abuses a child, then the child will not trust that adult. This is how one can tell the character and the personality of an adult, and whether or not he or she can be trusted with children.

The contribution of borrowed or foster children to the growth and prosperity of a new household is high in terms of economic production. The value of these children's participation is symbolized in the traditional marriage ceremony by presenting a boy and a girl to the new household. A child of each gender is presented in terms of the appropriate role. The Nilotic believe that early role association prepares the young to take their place in society. If a child has not been trained well, it is considered abuse. In this case, one has failed a child for life and can never be forgiven. If my niece Jam fails in her life, she will not be blamed. Rather, I will be considered a bad mother who abused my sister's child. If Jam succeeds, I will get credit for being a good mother. In this way, I show that I can be trusted with other children.

The Nilotic concept holds that adult women and men are fundamentally different from one another. Female and male adult roles are highly distinguished, and are set apart from one another by complex symbols, such as weapons, physical prowess, and either a tolerance for pain or susceptibility to it. The roles, activities, and life experiences of infant to pre-adolescent girls and boys, however, show only minor gender differences. Before puberty, gender roles are not strongly distinguished, but after puberty they are. This change in role expectations is marked for both genders by dramatic rites of initiation that signal the assumption of the status of a woman or a man. Initiation is considered the most significant event in the pre-adult life of the individual.

Initiation of boys is a communal ritual. The focal point of the ceremony is the operation of marking the forehead. During the operation, initiates must mask fear and pain and display courage and fortitude, or else suffer a loss of face in the community. The initiation ordeal is considered a test of the initiate's fitness for aspects of the adult role. Young men must display the courage befitting a warrior.

Initiation, particularly male initiation, is an important mark, not only of adult status but also of ethnic status. The operation of marking, as traditionally practiced by the Nilotic, is a one-time procedure. Boys are normally initiated between the ages of fourteen and fifteen. An initiation ceremony is conducted every year, though not necessarily every year in every community, and not necessarily in large or community wide ceremonies. Men of the community control the initiation ceremony for boys. Elders have important roles in the actual ceremony, but the planning and the instruction of initiates are in the hands of young men of the age-set immediately senior to the one being initiated. After the initiation ceremony, the nursing of the wounds is done by old women who have a reputation for their ritual knowledge. These women are considered pure, not engaging in sexual activity.

Initiation of girls is a more private matter. There is no communal ritual observed at the time of puberty for girls. The closest approximation to a female coming-of-age rite is when a girl has her first menses. She is then prohibited from drinking milk that comes from the general herd. Menstrual blood is believed to be dangerous to cattle, as it is thought to cause a cow to die or become barren. After the first menses, a particular cow is assigned to the girl. She and the cow together go through a ceremony that involves drinking milk and prayers from the elders. This ceremony is believed to nullify the effects of the menstrual pollution on the individual cow. Thereafter, the girl can drink milk only from that particular cow. She is encouraged to drink this milk, and the older women now tell her that she is a woman and must become strong.

With passage through puberty, the girl is considered sexually available and ready to go through a period of courtship. By age fifteen she is ready for marriage, and the recognition of mature womanhood. Courting couples are not supposed to engage in sexual intercourse. Ideally, a girl is a virgin at the time of her marriage. Brides who are virgins are held out as role models, and honored by the elders and the community at large. Nilotic girls are taught to believe that men are absolutely not to be trusted in sexual relationships. They are told that men take perverse pleasure in "ruining" girls, and in convincing girls to have intercourse by promising to marry them with no intention of following through.

The Initiation

Were the Duany boys initiated? I would say yes. Since we came to live in America, we have adapted to what people do here to mark the passage from youth to adulthood. Wal and I discovered that an equivalent American practice is to initiate young people through the ritual of driving school. The majority of young Americans have a driver's license by age sixteen, which is about the same age as a Nilotic young man would be initiated. When a young man gets behind the wheel of a motor vehicle, he assumes responsibility for himself, as well as for the other people on the road. We did not have spears or lion skins to give to the boys. Instead we gave them the car keys. We sent each of our children, both girls and boys, to driving school.

Athletic participation is another American initiation rite. For our family, basketball training has been like the Nilotic training of young warriors. Working out and playing the game has been a very hard training for our children. They worked hard everyday to perfect their skills and to become the best players. They also learned how to be team players.

The basketball arena was the scene of many tough times and many good times for the young Duanys. When one child's team won a game, we all celebrated. When one child's team lost a game, we all had to find ways to overcome the pain. Most families have a dish or two that is a sort of love medicine offered to a family member who is feeling a bit down or under the weather. The Duanys' favorite is warm milk and *legemat* (Sudanese donuts coated with powdered sugar). There is nothing like a big, round *legemat* drenched in warm milk. It comforts the spirit as well as the tummy.

Given the Hoosier madness for basketball, our children's height and ability began to turn the heads of elite universities as early as the seventh grade. Even though basketball fever reached a peak during the senior year of high school, academics were always at the top of all the little Duanys' programs. Mom and Dad said, "Study comes first. Remember that getting an education is what's important. You have to keep up with your school work and maintain at least a 3.0 average or else you cannot play basketball."

I am glad to say that each of the Duany children learned this lesson well: to do the schoolwork is to play basketball. Through their hard academic work and outstanding basketball performance, the young Duanys attracted attention from major university athletic programs all over the country.

Duany, our oldest son, received high school basketball awards on both the local and state levels. He received a full scholarship to play for the University of Wisconsin. His team made it to the national college basketball championship Final Four tournament in 2000. Duany studied behavioral science and pre-law. He continues to pursue a career in professional basketball.

Our oldest daughter Nyagon was a valedictorian of her high school class with a 4.00 grade point average. She was offered full scholarships in track and field, volleyball, and basketball. Nyagon accepted a full scholarship to play basketball for Bradley University. She is now a medical student at Indiana University.

Our second son Kueth has done it all. His high school basketball team, of which he was captain, won the state championship in 1997. Like his brother Duany, Kueth also received high school basketball awards on the local and state levels. He received a full scholarship to play for Syracuse University. Kueth was captain of his team when they won the 2003 NCAA college basketball championship title at New Orleans. Kueth is a double major in information science and political science.

Our youngest daughter Nok was a high school all-state selection in both basketball and volleyball. Nok was offered full scholarships in both volleyball and basketball. She accepted a full scholarship to play basketball for Georgetown University. She is studying marketing.

Bil, the youngest, is now in his final year of high school. Mom and Dad tell Bil what we told the others, "Do whatever it takes to win the game of basketball, and apply that same dedication toward getting an education. Once you get an education, nobody can ever take it away from you." We tell our children over and over that all this athletic recognition must be balanced with academic strength—and that is what any honest coach should say in recruiting students for university programs.

When it came time for Duany to choose a college, the recruiting game made us anxious, but we knew exactly what we wanted from the coaches and the athletic programs. Honesty was our number one priority, but it was sometimes hard to find. Every coach told us that his or her priority was academics, but the words were not always true.

Especially for the boys, the college basketball scene is a fiercely competitive environment. The pressure becomes more and more intense as the team advances toward the national playoffs. When Duany and Kueth played for teams that reached the Final Four games, we traveled as far as New Mexico and New Orleans to cheer them on to victory.

We wanted our children to be serious students, who would leave college with degrees and intellectual achievements. We had always placed the emphasis on working toward a degree, not just eligibility. We wanted a basketball coach who could promise to us that his or her students are going to attend classes regularly. Our insistence paid off. Our children have stayed in school.

We value education and our children know that very well. They know that we came halfway across the world, leaving our relatives, our friends, and the life we loved best to take advantage of the opportunities for education in the United States.

The passage to adulthood for the Duany children included rituals, training, study, and hard work. Wal and I succeeded in keeping our family on the right track because we applied Nilotic wisdom to what we found in the American environment. When I was growing up, my parents were there to encourage me. Their strength and experience were resources I could draw upon and build upon. This is how I came to understand that while my children were in my hands, it was mine to direct them in developing an exemplary character and to guide them in seeking a high purpose.

Beyond that, it is up to my children to spread their wings, to fly high, and to soar like young eagles.

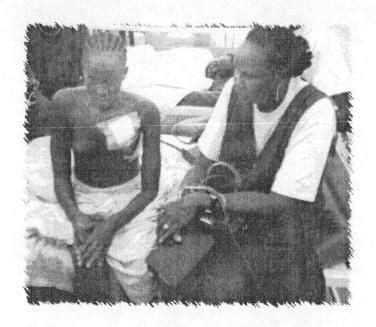

*With my niece Ayada at the Red
Cross hospital at Lokichokio, Kenya (1994)*

Chapter VII

The Nightmare

The main source of instability and suffering of the southern Sudanese and many other African refugees is no longer a war of independence, but brutal civil and guerrilla armed conflicts. The results are wide spread ethnic conflicts. Humanitarian services for refugee and displaced people have been politicized and militarized beyond recognition. This serious breakdown of human values offers no glimmer of hope for people in southern Sudan, or in many other parts of Africa.

I Return Home

When I was living in Africa, I learned from reading books that America was a land of great busyness and great opportunity. The images that formed in my imagination were of Americans enjoying warm homes or living on the open range, all with a healthy undercurrent of humor. I also learned from books about certain Americans who had contempt for the less fortunate and attempted to do them injury. Books told me that men such as John D. Rockefeller, Henry Ford, Andrew Carnegie, and other great industrialists were thieves. I did not believe this message. If these men were such bad people, why then did they give away so much of their money to help other people? The story of

John Rockefeller is the story of many European-Americans. He was born poor on a farm; he believed that through industry and hard work he could succeed in life.

I am not a European-American, but I was one of the lucky ones who received an African Dissertation Internship Award from the Rockefeller Foundation. The award enabled me to return briefly to Sudan. In 1993, I went to Khartoum, Nairobi, and southern Sudan, where I saw first hand what had been happening during the nine years I had been away. It would be an understatement to say that I was stunned.

Islamic *Jihad*

Since Sudan's beginning as an independent state in 1956, except for ten years of peace (1972-1983), open warfare between the North and the South has been the standard. The Islamic Arab North has maintained tight economic, educational, and military control over the South. A shattering act of genocide came in 1983, when the Islamist revolutionaries in Khartoum under President Gaafar Mohammed Nimeiry declared the *Shari'a*—traditional Islamic Law—to be the civil law of Sudan.

Once the Islamist revolutionaries took control of the country, they turned Sudan into an Islamic State and Khartoum into an Islamist Mecca. *Iq'tul el Kufaar* (kill the infidels) is often repeated in the market places and in the mosques. Mass murder, religious cleansing, torture, starvation, rape, abduction, and forced labor are acts of Islamist heroism. Do these cruelties epitomize a true follower of Allah? I don't believe so.

Sudanese young men who fight in the *Jihad*— in the defense of Islam—are promised a heavenly reward. I am told that every man who offers his life for Islam is assured that seventy virgins will receive him into heaven! He dies believing that seventy virgins await his pleasure. When I heard that, I asked myself, "What heavenly reward shall a woman find? Will she be received by seventy lusty men?" Most women I know would run from a "heaven" like that! I would.

To escape the destruction of the southern liberation armies, large numbers of southern Sudanese children fled to the North. But in the desert cities of the North, they are no better off. Children of southern Sudan become street children in the northern towns. They can receive charity only when they convert to Islam. Denied affection, education, and assistance, these children survive by their own wits. They are experts in crime and violence. Many are caught by the police and tried as criminals under Islamic law. They face amputation or some other cruel method of punishment.

African girls as young as eight years old are used for sexual pleasure within the Arab communities where they live. There are no laws to protect them from abuse. These girls also are forced to submit to certain rituals. In one, the genitals of a young girl are mutilated according to Arab custom, in a procedure known as female circumcision. This is not practiced in southern Sudanese communities. In Khartoum I saw with my own eyes little southern Sudanese girls who had been subjected to this ritual. The tender parts of their genitals had been cut away and the wound crudely stitched closed—all without anesthesia. This is a female ritual among the Arabs that has its origin in generations past. It is passed down from grandmother to mother to daughter. It is a treacherous heirloom, an unforgettable wound that slices open a young girl's soul and creates a pain she will carry all her life. No other person can understand the deep pain of these women, except those who have had similar experiences.

Jabal al Awliya Displaced Camp

A 1994 Human Rights Watch report states that 4.7 million people live in Sudan, but 20 percent of the total population have been displaced. I am one of the displaced, but I am one of the lucky ones. I eventually found myself living in Bloomington, Indiana, with a family of nine: my husband, five children, a niece, and a nephew.

The magnitude of the problem of the displaced population is something nobody understands better than do the Sudanese people. The report states that in the rural South, 80 percent of the children are malnourished and one out of six is at risk of starvation. There is no healthcare and no education. An entire generation of children in the South has grown to maturity without education. Villages have become ghost villages. My family is fortunate. But what about the displaced living in the refugee camps?

This question never left my mind while I was in Khartoum in April 1993. That is why I visited a displaced camp near the village of Jabal al Awliya, south of Khartoum. This camp is one of forty-eight camps around the city. The village of Jabal al Awliya used to have a busy fish market. Now Jabal al Awliya is a place where people have completely lost their way of life. At the time of my visit, this one camp alone provided shelter for over 50,000 southern Sudanese who had fled their homes because of the civil war.

On the day of my visit to the displaced camp, my niece Thongdiar and I arrived in central Khartoum at 7:00 a.m., hoping to catch a truck to Jabal al Awliya. We heard a man yelling, *"Jabal al Awliya, al Jabal, al Jabal."* Quietly, my niece and I walked to the truck and got on. It was very crowded; people were seated shoulder to shoulder. The majority of the passengers were the Arab nomads who sell their farm products in the city and then return to their villages. People, animals, birds, were all packed together in the small space. We could hardly move. A truck that should have carried only 12 passengers was now carrying 25-30 people, plus their belongings.

After having lived for years in America where life is comfortable and public transportation is efficient, I was shocked. Here I had to struggle to find a small place for my feet. I tried very hard to settle in. This was not new to me. I had ridden these trucks before, and I knew I could do it again. But after living in relative comfort for so long, it required some effort.

I thought I was ready to do whatever it took to reach the displaced camp. I wanted to see the refugee situation with my own eyes. But as the truck began to move, I began to wonder, "Why am I doing this? What in the world was my reason for taking such a risk? Where did this idea of going to Jabal al Awliya come from?"

As I sat deep in thought, my niece asked me in Dinka, *"Ee ngu malet cin biet*? Why are you so quiet, Aunt?"

I peeked out from under my head-covering and smiled at her, *"Acin kidaa.* Nothing," I said.

It took us an hour and a half on a bumpy dirt road to reach Jabal al Awliya. Upon our arrival at the Arab village of Jabal al Awliya, the truck suddenly stopped. In seconds it was surrounded by soldiers screaming at the passengers, *"Anzil kula kum!* Get down now, everybody!" We were so frightened that my niece and I found ourselves tightly gripping each other's hands. I was afraid that the soldiers would recognize us as outsiders because my niece and I were obviously healthier than the women who lived in the camp were. If we were exposed, my niece and I would be arrested and taken back to Khartoum. I began to sweat like crazy, and tried to stay calm.

In every village and town in Sudan there are checkpoints where crude soldiers push and pull the passengers around in search of weapons. Because of the lack of security, the soldiers are very hostile, intent on intimidating the passengers. At the village of Jabal al Awliya, the soldiers checked all bags and baskets on the truck. After all had been inspected, the passengers were released.

I stood helpless beside the truck, still questioning why I had come to the camp. Then we were ordered to get back on the vehicle. I was very happy that we had escaped notice by these soldiers. One soldier yelled, *"Ya la, ya la.* Go, go," and the truck started going. After a few minutes it reached the village market place. Thongdiar and I got down and started walking towards the camp, which was three miles distant. As we passed through the Arab village, we saw in front of a hut, a girl braiding a woman's hair. They could have been mother and daughter. We saw an old lady killing a rooster in the yard behind her house. The rooster escaped her grasp and ran around headless until it collapsed in the middle of the road. We stepped over the bloody trail, watching as the lady picked up the dead bird. She greeted us, *"Salaam."* This is the Arabic word, peace.

The sun is intense in the Sahara Desert; on this day the temperature was 115°F. Everybody had something on his or her head to shield the sun's rays, even if it were no more than a little piece of cloth. There were no trees, and not even a twig of wood on the ground.

As we approached the south side of the camp we saw a place where they put the dirt; it was the *zibala* (garbage dump). When we passed by the *zibala*, we saw dogs, goats, sheep, and donkeys from a nearby Arab village searching for something to eat. It was also a place where the children of Jabal al Awliya's displaced camp had come to search for something edible. I imagined my own children climbing over the filth. Tears rolled down my cheeks. I quickly wiped my face so that my niece wouldn't see me crying. I didn't want to break her heart. I wanted to show her that I was strong. I bowed my head and prayed with all my heart, "O, God grant me the serenity to accept the things I cannot change, the courage to change the things I can, and the wisdom to know the difference."

Still sobbing, I raised my head. We were already in the camp. There were many ethnic groups of people in the camp; the majority were Dinka Ngong, of the Abyei area of the southern Durfur Region in western Sudan. These were the people of Deng Majok, a very well known Dinka chief.

"Where are Deng Majok's children?" my niece asked. "Aren't these their people?"

Every Sudanese knew of Chief Deng Majok; even little Dinka children in far away lands had heard his name. He was well known because he had two hundred wives. Many of his children were well-educated, and some had married European or American women. Unfortunately, many of Deng

193

Majok's numerous children left their villages and never came back to their homeland. Now there was no one to help their own Dinka people.

"One of Deng Majok's children is a well-known scholar in the United States," I said. "He has written several books about the Sudanese. He is a great scholar, but not in a way that benefits his own people."

My niece, who was still puzzled as to why the Dinka Ngong had ended up in the displaced camp, asked, "Doesn't he care about his own people? Who reads his books any way?"

"American and European people." I said.

"What about his own people?"

"None of them read his books," I replied. "His books are not written for his own people."

I told Thongdiar I didn't know what was wrong with some Africans. I didn't understand why educated Africans did not go back home and help their people. We thought of many leaders of Africa, such as Jumo Kenyatta, Julius Nyerere, Jamal Abul Nasir, and Kwame Nkrumah, who went to the West to get an education and returned to their countries to share their knowledge with their own people. Thongdiar and I knew of no educated child of Deng Majok who was prepared to become a chief. This realization was a moment of despair for my young niece and me. We were quiet as we walked further into the camp.

Soon we noticed a weak looking woman in her mid or late thirties. Near her sat a frail little boy of about four. My niece greeted her in Dinka, "*Cii yi baak!* Good afternoon!"

"*Heen cii bak.* Good afternoon," she replied. We asked if we could sit with her for a moment. She agreed. We introduced ourselves as Dinka women from Bahr el Gazal region, now living in the city of

Khartoum. We told her that we had come to visit the camp. She was very happy to meet us. We could see the surprise in her face as she asked how we had gotten in to Jabal al Awliya. We were shocked to learn that her tiny son was really six years old. The lady accompanied us as we walked through part of the camp.

We saw many unexpected things happening in this sparse, dusty place. Right in front of our eyes we saw a woman in labor. An old woman tried to chase the children away from the site. *"Nyai ke root, nyai ke root!"* she screamed. "Get away, get away!" To the pack of curious youngsters it was a fun game: the young teasing the old. The children obviously enjoyed every minute of it, skipping about in the desert heat, streams of sweat running down their dusty, naked bodies. Sweat dripped from their hair into their eyes. They shook their heads like dogs after swimming in the Nile, spraying water everywhere. I marveled that despite these horrible conditions, the children had not lost their natural ability to explore, to enjoy, to fear, and to be tantalized. These little ones were innocent. They had no place to play and did not understand the reality of the day.

In Nilotic communities, a woman in labor is well taken care of. Her privacy is very important. But in the Jabal al Awliya displaced camp there was no shelter to offer privacy. Thongdiar and I witnessed the birth of a Sudanese child right out in the open. Not five feet away two men sat on a scrap of cardboard for a mat. One of the men was very sick with malaria fever.

All over the camp, I heard the voices of little children crying because they were either sick or hungry. I had not met any of these people before, yet walking among them didn't give me an uneasy feeling.

Walking among them helped me to become more intensely aware of their suffering. This experience has become my living nightmare. And it compels me to pray now, as I did when I walked through the camp, "War is stupid. This must stop. Peace must come."

There was no sanitation in the camp and we saw human waste and swarms of flies everywhere. The lack of toilet facilities was a serious problem, which some people had tried to solve by using plastic bags as toilets. These plastic bags had once contained life-saving relief supplies. On the bags were printed words like, Made in USA, or Made in UK, or Canada, or Holland, or Germany, or even Taiwan. Now the writing stamped on the bags conveyed something hideous.

I thought about some of the charity advertisements I had seen on American television and said jokingly to my niece, "These bags would make a good product for the charity organizations to promote. The announcer would say, 'Please send us your money so we can buy multi-purpose bags for the refugees.' Then the relief worker would lift a bag filled with waste up to the camera and say, "'Strong enough to hold anything!'"

The bags were covered with flies.

When the Western media reports international news, they like to illustrate the stories with images of famine, refugees, and displaced people. I had seen many of these heartbreaking images on television and in newspapers. The disasters and wars in the reports are noted by the Western public, but the suffering is so very far away that viewers and readers in America have no connection to the relentless reality. After a few minutes, the reporter turns to other stories, the reader picks up another section of newspaper, and life goes on.

In Jabal al Awliya displaced camp, I couldn't escape the sights, the sounds, and the smells. I couldn't change the channel. I couldn't throw away the newspaper. This was not the news. This was life. This was a nightmare, and I was right in the center of it.

Civil war in Sudan has destroyed a people's way of life and has resulted in death, famine, starvation, epidemic disease, and a large population of displaced people. The majority who suffer are women and children. They are victims of persecution, exploitation, and violence.

I still ask myself: Why is this? What can be done to stop the war? Will life ever go back to normal? Will peace ever come to Sudan?

I don't know.

The Liberation Movement

From Khartoum I flew to Nairobi, Kenya. From there I went into southern Sudan for a few days.

Ten years of civil war had turned all of Sudan into a disaster area, but in the South the situation was desperate. Together, the Sudanese government and the Sudan People's Liberation Army/Movement (SPLA/M) had plunged the people into chaos. Southern Sudan had become a battlefield. Villages were destroyed; entire communities were uprooted and relocated into displaced camps. In response to the disaster they were creating, both the government and the SPLA/M had created their own relief programs and were courting the Western world to provide relief assistance. They now were competing for the few resources available from the United Nations and other non-governmental organizations (NGOs). For the West, this situation simply was more evidence that African people could not govern themselves and needed their old masters back.

The humanitarian crisis was entirely man-made. Southern Sudan has rich natural resources and a diverse food production system. Before this war, most people lived well on milk from their cattle, on the vegetables they grew, and on the wild game and fish they caught. People knew how to survive lean years. But they have no defense against man-made famine. In man-made famine, where people are not allowed to produce food, people starve in the face of plenty. Both the Islamist government and the SPLA/M use famine-induced genocide to subdue the population. They know that by deliberately starving people and forcing them to leave their villages in search of food, they defeat the will and the strength of the people to rise up in defense of their most basic human rights. The immorality of man-made famine is beyond comprehension. It kills not only the body, but also destroys the spirit, as well as the culture, its institutions, and ways of life.

When the population of an area is inundated with a displaced population in search of relief food, epidemics of small pox, dysentery, influenza, typhus, malaria, yellow fever, typhoid fever, tuberculosis, Kala-Azar, syphilis, and HIV/AIDS follow. Famine and epidemic disease strike hardest among the women and children.

In southern Sudan, one third of all newborn babies die. The vast majority of those who survive infancy will not live to see their fifth birthday. Death is a constant companion of southern Sudanese children. Girls and boys know that as they walk through the woods and grass, any step they take could activate a land mine. Day and night, children of all ages listen for the sound of airplanes—and the bombs that inevitably follow. The children are always on guard, ready to hide from southern faction raiding parties that have come to burn their village, take their food, rape the girls and women, and kill or kidnap the young men.

The Government of Sudan, however, did not cause the worst devastation in the South. Great injury was caused by the SPLA/M imposing its rendition of Marxist-Leninist doctrine upon the people. Before the SPLA/M split in 1991, the liberation army controlled 90 per cent of the rural areas. The SPLA/M had strong support from Colonel Mengistu Haile Mariam's regime in Ethiopia, as well as from the African socialist countries, Cuba, and the Soviet Eastern Bloc countries.

Military training camps and control centers were established at the border villages in southern Sudan. Most of the fighters were young southern Sudanese boys who were forcefully taken into the guerrilla forces. Many stayed on voluntarily, liking the life of an armed bandit better than the drudgery of peasant farming. Others found guerrilla life difficult and tried to escape. Only a few succeeded. Those caught trying to flee were executed, which served as a strong deterrent to others. One of the most cruel actions of the liberation movement was the killing of child soldiers as young as eight years old.

The SPLA/M was trying to create a new generation for the New Sudan. I met many young men who had survived the coercive rule of SPLA/M. While living under the movement's control, they had learned to cope with life under a brutal security system. Many of those who escaped became the street children in Nairobi or Khartoum. These able young men, who were willing to work to make the South a better place, ended up sitting doing nothing in refugee camps, living only to be fed by the World Food Program (WFP).

In their effort to destabilize and control the South, SPLA/M cut off food to rural areas in order to cause hardship to the population, who in turn were deceived into aiming their frustration and fury at the Sudan government. SPLA/M forces burned crops in the fields and destroyed local farmers' grain. They put land mines on the roads to prevent relief lorries from reaching the villages. Local people caught trying to flee to the North to find food were brutally killed. By August 1989, conditions in the villages had deteriorated to the point that there was famine throughout most of southern Sudan. That is when the United Nations started to airdrop food into the areas controlled by SPLA/M. Generally, the food went first to feed SPLA/M soldiers.

Some of the airdrops contained more than food intended for the starving populace. Among the sacks of grain were hidden boxes of war supplies. The Norwegian Peoples Aid (NPA), which operates outside the United Nations, was the primary agency transporting war materials to the SPLA/M. Many local people reported to me that the NPA used their planes to drop war supplies instead of relief supplies. Some boxes in the airdrops contained land mines that ended up in the roads to destroy food relief lorries or in the fields to stop people from cultivating. Hungry people who came to the drop area expecting food were given nothing. They saw instead that the SPLA/M's supporters were engaged in supplying war materials while people all over southern Sudan were starving to death.

The idea of humanitarian aid became a cruel joke. Local people called the United Nation's Operation Life Line Sudan (UN/OLS) "Operation Loot Sudan." Once I asked a smiling relief worker why OLS was unable to get the food into the hands of the people. The smile vanished from his face and he said, "Because nothing works here. Because this is f—ing Africa. Because those f—ing soldiers, those f—ing irrational people, are not worth our f—ing energy."

I understood why the relief worker was so frustrated. In ten years my homeland had descended into chaos. The liberation movement had destroyed the social structures of the society. Countless people had died. Over four million had been made refugees and the majority of southern Sudanese were either directly or indirectly affected by the war. But what the relief worker did not understand was that terrorist, guerrilla tactics were not the normal African way of getting things done.

The relief worker had never experienced what life was like before the liberation movement tried to re-make the southern Sudanese society. But I knew a time when people in southern Sudan embodied those most notable characteristics of resourcefulness and self-reliance. Before they were driven off their land, the local people carried self-reliance to a high art. Now, I feared, it was to become a lost art. In southern Sudan, cohesive indigenous or linguistic groups are the only transmitters of cultural capital from one generation to the next. Had ten years of chaos completely destroyed our link to our past?

I Return to Nairobi

After my first visit to Sudan in April 1993, I knew that I had to return. I had to find out more. I had to find some way to bring peace.

In 1994, I flew from Bloomington to Nairobi, Kenya. As soon as I stepped off the plane, my younger brother Ater and his wife said, "You have to go to our sister! The SPLA attacked her village. They hurt one of her children." The following morning, I caught a United Nations flight to Lokichokio, the UN base of operations in northern Kenya. I went to the Red Cross hospital where my niece, Ayada, was being treated.

It was a hospital of more than 1,200 patients, all victims of inter-factional fighting among the rival liberation movement armies. I hadn't seen Ayada for ten years. Would I know her? She was only six years old when I left Sudan, Now she was a young woman. As I walked through the hospital, looking for Ayada, an old woman from our village recognized me and yelled, "Oh, there is Aker!" Everyone who could get up came running to see me. Ayada was among them. All of us were in tears. Ayada showed me the place where the bullet from an SPLA assault rifle had entered her body. Her left breast was gone but, thank God, Ayada was alive.

As I write these words, two million southern Sudanese men, women, and children have perished, and more are going to die if the war does not stop. It is only by the grace of God that I am alive to be able to write and to speak for the voiceless millions of southern Sudanese people who are being trampled underfoot in a ruthless struggle for power and riches.

Back in Nairobi, I found many refugees from southern Sudan. Among them was Nyankiir, a refugee woman struggling to survive in an unfriendly city. I sat in Nyankiir's bare living room. Her face was ashen as she spoke in low, desperate tones. "I lost my husband," she began to sob. "I can't go on."

"You must go on," I replied quietly. "You have five children to raise."

"But how will I find food, clothing, education, healthcare, and all that it takes to make a life? I just can't go on."

I tried to explain to her that the strength to face the difficulties of life lay in herself and in the God who created her. She was so obsessed with her grief, however, that she could not listen. A year later I heard that Nyankiir had developed heart disease and died. I really think she died of a broken heart. Nyankiir is typical of the many southern Sudanese women who are confronted with the trauma of civil war. I knew all along the only medicine that could cure Nyankiir's condition was peace, but I did not have peace in my hands to give her.

Nyankiir's husband had been a commander in the SPLA. Like many southern Sudanese, he had a heart for the southern people. He wanted to fight for the liberation of southern Sudan. One day out in the bush he became ill, but the SPLA would not send him to a doctor for treatment. By the time he finally was sent to Nairobi, it was too late for the doctors to do anything and he died. There are many southern Sudanese who have lost their lives this way. These were well-meaning people who spent their whole lives committed to a just cause, but who, all along, were used and manipulated by a self-serving organization. In the end, Nyankiir and her children were abandoned by the organization her husband had served.

I spoke to many other refugee women in Nairobi. I heard the same stories of loss and abandonment, and experienced the same frustration of not knowing what to say. I could not tell a woman whose husband had been killed, "He will come back." I could not tell a mother whose child was sick, "She will get well." What then, could I say to these women? It was only through the hope of peace that I could say anything at all to them. I could only offer my own hope that someday we will find a way to change things for the better.

That's what I believe. Despite everything I have seen and heard of the suffering of my people, despite the loss my own family has experienced, the seed of hope still lives within me. Is it not from dirty, nauseating humus that green plants sprout into life? Likewise, from the soil of human suffering, I can feel new growth of hope springing up within me.

I gave my word to those women: "There will be peace. We will find a way. I will never stop searching for it."

My Own Nightmare

The nightmares in Sudan that I was told about are not dreams. They are real. Mothers watch their children starve to death. Young boys are forced to shoot their parents as an initiation into SPLA/M; women die in labor because there are no doctors or midwives to help. I heard countless horror stories. I saw the suffering. I have my own nightmares.

In early 1985, at the beginning of the civil war, I lost my two younger brothers: Machar (a stepbrother) who was only 17 years old, and Makuac (Augustine) who was 19. Also, Wal and I know that many of our friends and colleagues are now dead. In many cases, we learned the details of how they lost their lives. Everyone from southern Sudan has nightmares that haunt him or her. In southern Sudan, every family has lost at least one or two family members in this war.

Brutal, inter-factional fighting among southern liberation movements has shattered the lives of the people. The liberation armies rule by terrorizing the people in the countryside and driving families from their homes. The self-proclaimed Sudan People's Liberation Army is not a grassroots army arising from the people. Instead, it descended upon them like a plague of locusts, and then broke into warring factions.

As a mother, I came to realize that the Sudan People's Liberation Movement offered no future for the young generation. I know that the future of southern Sudan is not with a movement. It is with the young people, whom the movement has killed or abandoned or uprooted from villages. Both the SPLA/M and the Government of Sudan routinely abduct civilians. Children are prize catches. The SPLA/M needs boys and young men to fill its ranks; the Arabs need laborers to work in their fields. I have talked with many children, and I know the situation in the South. It is a place of terror; it is a place of death.

It is easy for me to see that the money used to buy machine guns and land mines should have been invested in food production, health care, and education. It is easy for me to understand the value of peace. But the younger generation of Sudanese has been taught that they can build a future for themselves with the tools of destruction. In blindly following political saviors, the young generation has forged the very chains that now bind them to lives of violence and poverty. What trouble we Sudanese have created! It is very difficult to unchain people's minds from the shackles of war, especially when individual Sudanese government army officers and SPLA Comrades (as they like to call themselves) are becoming enormously rich in money, cattle, sheep, goats, and women that they have taken by force from the very people they claim to be liberating!

In 1995, I went to Washington, D.C. I went to the American Vietnam War Memorial. The memorial consists of two long, adjoining black granite walls inscribed with the names of the 58,000 dead and missing U.S. soldiers who fought in the civil war in Vietnam. It is not a monument to victory. It is a tombstone. Most visitors reach out and touch the inscribed names. Many have tears in their eyes. A similar memorial built in Sudan would be *nearly thirty times longer* than the one in Washington. Such a memorial will never be built. If we asked the Comrades for the names of the dead, we would find no record of the individual, human cost of this war. The Comrades would tell us, "This is the high price we all must pay for the liberation."

But all are not paying the price. The Comrades are comfortably removed from the field of battle. They live in luxury homes in the suburbs of Nairobi and Kampala. Even when they go to the jungles of southern Sudan, they bring along the comforts of home and cases of Johnny Walker whisky. The masses fight while they relax, sipping whisky and listening to Western music. It is not the Comrades, but rather the common people—our loved ones—who are paying the price of the liberation.

The dialectic of the Comrades makes me wonder if they aren't writing a sequel to George Orwell's *Animal Farm*. In Orwell's parable, the

Animal Farm pigs preach liberation and equality, wooing the less clever animals into following their noble cause. All of the farm animals take part in the struggle, but ultimately it is Napoleon, the most ruthless of the pigs, who rises to the top and lives in luxury. He and his comrade pigs consume all that is produced by the other animals. The animal's dream of freedom and prosperity becomes a nightmare. While the book may not be well known in Africa, its tragic message is very familiar to those who are experiencing the reality. In the Comrade's world, everyone is equal, and some will always be more equal than others.

Today, many voices are leading the Sudanese people down paths, both ancient and modern, lined with promises of a better future. Indeed, all of Africa desperately struggles to find a better way of life. The Islamist revolutionaries promise Sudan a better future, but it is a future that will cost the South its soul. The actions of the Islamists have caused the southern Sudanese to lose all trust in the North. The path to the ancient Islamic order leads to subjugation.

The Sudan People's Liberation Movement also promises Sudan a better future, but the reality they have created reveals that their hope is false. They have given the South hunger, terror, and destruction. They have condemned the southern Sudanese people to perpetual poverty. They have either killed or driven away nearly everyone who has education and experience. The path to the modern Marxist paradise leads straight to hell on earth.

There must be a better way.
There must be an end to this nightmare.

Julia Aker Duany

Mary Nyakang Chol (Nyachol), a leader of one of the women's groups,
speaking at one of the grassroots peace conferences in Upper Nile.

Chapter VIII

Making Peace

Peace is a group effort. Nilotic women take the peace so seriously that it becomes the affair of everyone of them.

When it comes to matters of the heart, the lazy laughter of Nilotic women transforms into a spiral of opinion that rises like smoke from a fire. It is matter of the heart to say it as it is, and to say it all in order to stop conflict. Telling the truth is what makes the Nilotic people the way they are. They are very open people.

Women as Truth Seekers

In early 1993, inter-factional fighting among the SPLM/A groups was escalating at an alarming rate, drawing the communities into the armed violence. The cycle of injury and retaliation reached a peak in the Upper Nile Region near Nasir and Akobo, as the Lou and Jikany Nuer clans clashed over fishing, grazing, and water rights. The local bandits took full advantage of the breakdown of law and order, and both Nuer clans lost many of their animals to rustlers. Both clans were well supplied with modern weapons, resulting in staggering losses of life. More than 1,300 people died; 150,000 people were displaced, and over 300 homes burned. This was the first time in the history of the

Nuer that clan had turned upon clan without restraint, destroying property and killing women, children, and the elderly.

In January 1994, I visited Nasir, a small town about 200 miles east of Malakal, the capital of Upper Nile State. I have relatives in this area, because my father came from the Lou. I arrived to find the Jikany Nuer rebuilding their homes after an attack from the Lou Nuer. I stayed in Nasir for two weeks, discussing issues of concern and planning self-help programs with women's groups.

During my visit, I witnessed the suffering of the people. Every day I heard told in my own language horrifying stories. The outpouring of stories from the women became like removing the layers of a great, narrative onion. One story peeled off only to uncover another. The more I listened, the more I learned, and the more deeply I felt the pain. The stories painted a vivid picture of the social circumstances in which the Nilotic people live today.

But I not only heard about the suffering. I experienced life in the war zone of southern Sudan right alongside the women. I slept in the huts, was bitten by the mosquitoes, went hungry, and crouched in the bunkers during aerial bombings. I was not used to these sudden aerial attacks. Whenever an attack occurred, the shock and fear nearly overcame my senses.

On my first day in Nasir, I became so disturbed by what I heard and saw that I felt sick to my stomach. What had become of the life that I left behind? The stories from the women rang like blows to my head. In each story words such as shooting, killing, rape, and blood came from the women's mouths. There was so much blood. Blood ran in every story. That night I refused to eat anything. Neither could I sleep. The next day, the women told me that I had not yet heard the worst.

I was told that SPLA took boys as young as five into the Red Army and as a form of initiation forced them to either witness or participate in brutal executions. Violence had become admirable, manly behavior. Indeed, the young men and boys, as taught by the liberation movement, had come to identify themselves through violent deeds. Armed with AK-47 machine guns, they demonstrated their manhood by raiding villages, looting homes, raping women, and stealing cattle. Gangs of young boys would gather to raid their neighbors just for fun. As these trained killers attacked villages, they would shout their war slogans and war cries at top of their voices, *"SPLA wee yee! SPLA wee yee!"* Out for blood, these young boys struck and stabbed at the little children, the helpless old people, and anyone not able to run away. Boys who killed the most people and who showed no fear were regarded as heroes by the liberation movement and singled out to become group leaders.

People hid from these gangs in the tall savanna grass, or in the air raid bunkers, or behind big trees in the jungle. If the gangs didn't kill their captives, they generally tortured them.

The SPLA soldiers also tortured their captives. The soldiers were to eliminate the people they deemed "useless".

One day a tall, wisp of a woman began telling me how much she missed her home. While she spoke, she slowly made motions with her hands, showing me how she had milked her cows. *"Ca ngach hak mit along,"* she said. "I miss milking my cows very much."

I supposed that the woman could not weigh more than sixty pounds. Her soft voice buzzed like a mosquito in my ear. I closed my eyes. It was like a bad dream. This woman had no cows to milk. Now she was starving and forced to eat the relief food. Now her existence was flavored with bitterness such that her grandmother and her great-grandmother had never tasted.

I thought of my childhood and of the cattle camp where we had once filled our stomachs with milk. The Nilotic peoples measure wealth primarily in terms of cattle. A man who has no cattle is *aa toch,* looked down upon as having very low social status. And though the war has devastated, displaced, and disrupted economic activity, the criteria for judging social merit has not changed. Concern for cattle still permeates Nilotic life in social matters. Cattle are still essential for paying bridewealth and making restitution.

The relative merits and well being of the cattle are still a major preoccupation among the Nilotic people. Young men of the warrior age-set still watch the herds. A young Nilotic man will risk his life to save one of his animals. In the present climate of lawlessness, the cycle of raiding cattle and retaliation has become an endless affair, blood for blood. Countless young herdsmen have lost their lives simply defending their cattle.

Some years ago I read a book that an early colonial officer had written about the Nilotic people of East Africa. He believed that people who tended cattle did not do any work at all. He had observed the young Nilotic men passing their days in "idleness." To the colonial officer, a man squatting on a rock gazing at cattle or standing on one leg whistling to cattle was a man doing nothing. The officer could not understand that the men he saw actually were working, and that they bore a great responsibility. Tending cattle is peace to Nilotic men. It is a way of nurturing life. And this is why a man or a boy is prepared to die to save his animals. They are his life.

But when I was in Nasir in 1994, the cattle were gone. I now saw living empty lives in they eyes of people whom I had known since childhood. The bonds of memory that I should have enjoyed with those who had shared the games of my childhood were broken by the intervening violence.

One morning I sat under a tree among a group of women, listening as they talked. For some reason, I noticed the sun shining as I have never before known the sun to shine. Leila Reth, one of the leaders of women in Nasir, began describing the sufferings of her home village. She told how women there had come together to make peace. Tears rolled down her cheeks as she asked the women of Nasir to come together and stop the fighting.

Next, a woman with a trembling voice began to address the group:

> *Mäle mi goa Nyiiri!* Peace upon you ladies! Peace is a phrase we hear from everyone in Nuer country. It is deeply rooted in our culture. We are praying everyday so that fighting will not happen here again. Ladies, you must start the peace from your homes. We have to work hard to have peace among ourselves in order to farm and keep our animals. For a Nuer, life without cattle

seems worthless, so peace must be kept."

Another woman described the attack on her village in which she lost her two children:

"It was five o'clock in the morning when, I heard the first gun shot. I thought it was the government army attacking. Within a short time, there were dead bodies everywhere. There was a lot of confusion because of the smoke from the burning huts. We ran this way, others that way, but there was no way out. Two of my children were shot that day. One died on the spot and the other one died later, because he lost all his blood. Houses and food supplies were burnt, and the whole community fled the area. After about ten hours, the liberation movement, [South Sudan Independence Movement (SSIM/A) led by Riek Machar], brought in their army and restored order. They tried to encourage those who had fled to return to the town, but not many did. That is why you find us here."

As the layers of stories fell away, I discovered at the very heart of each one the persistence of women as the center of life. This hidden fullness of the heart was not visible to outsiders, but I recognized it because it was characteristic of the day-to-day life of southern Sudanese communities that I remembered. Through their stories, the women reflected upon their traditional role as wives and mothers, and also upon their new role as breadwinners.

The talk moved on from the horror and the difficulties that so many had suffered to emphasize life, the need to farm and fish, and to gather wild plants and fruit. These life-sustaining activities could not be done in the midst of civil war and ethnic fighting. Life, to southern Sudanese women, is peace. This theme began to appear consistently, from story to story and from woman to woman. It became clear to all of us that peace means more than the absence of fighting. Peace is a total way of life.

Discovering a Hidden Truth

In African societies, women and men play different roles, have access to different resources, and bear different responsibilities. Among the southern Sudanese, especially the Nuer, women traditionally have had a significant role to play in maintaining stability in their communities through bringing conflicting parties together. I wanted to encourage both Jikany and Lou women to seek peace and reconciliation within their communities. I felt that as a Sudanese woman, I had a duty to promote the traditional processes of conflict resolution and to raise peace awareness among the women.

Later in 1994, after I had finished my dissertation, I returned to southern Sudan specifically to organize women to work for peace. My approach was to involve women directly in the process of peace making, building upon the woman's role as a mother and as a member of her community. I reasoned that lasting change in the life of people could come through creative application of their own values, derived from their own unique social context.

Women were quick to grasp the concept of maintaining peace by reclaiming their traditional role of pressuring antagonists to sit down and discuss their problems. Their small successes gave the local people confidence in the women's efforts. As the women's efforts expanded into more villages, incidents of ethnic conflict diminished. The emergence of a grassroots peace, rather than of a peace imposed from the top down, surprised the SPLA/M leadership. In a short time, the localized efforts of the women began to take on the characteristics of a broader, grassroots movement.

In fact, after the 1991 SPLA/M split localized grassroots peace initiatives to counter the fighting among the liberation movement factions had begun emerging in the Upper Nile Region of southern Sudan as early as 1992. The Dinka, however, had the upper hand in suppressing any real or perceived opposition from the Nuer and other groups, because they controlled the SPLA/M.

Several external peace groups also had organized to find ways to end the factional violence. The most notable, perhaps, is the Inter-Governmental Authority on Drought and Development (IGADD), formed by the member states Ethiopia, Eritrea, Jibuti, Kenya, Somalia, Sudan, Uganda, and the Carter Center for Peace (USA). All of these external efforts failed to make headway because they lacked understanding of both the underlying issues and the indigenous processes of conflict resolution.

What made the difference in my work with women in 1994 was the individual readiness of a majority of southern Sudanese women to act. My words would have amounted to nothing without the community-wide participation of women, their understanding of which approaches could be successful and why, and their strong faith in their own traditional ways of solving problems.

The solidarity of the women gave birth to a spirit of reconciliation among the Lou and the Jikany communities. The authority of the women in pushing antagonists toward discussion and telling the truth was not questioned or challenged. The Nilotic people honored this authority because the Nilotic woman is perceived as *maan Naath,* mother of the nation, and she is expected to do things correctly. This ideal has always been a charge to women, and they are expected to live up to it.

Although both men and women are taught from childhood about the value of honesty and truth telling, mothers are the primary teachers of this value to their young. A story with a universal theme that Nilotic mothers have handed down to their children is this tale about the boy who told lies:

> A boy was watching the cattle near the village. Occasionally he called "*Ci lony ben! Ci lony ben!* The lion is coming!" Men grabbed their spears and ran to protect the herd. When he saw the men running, the boy laughed and told them that there was no lion. He did it several times, and one day when the real lion attacked the cattle, nobody came to rescue him, because no one believed him any longer.

A stable society depends upon truth in relationships. How well a woman lives out her responsibility for bringing out truth in the family greatly shapes her circumstances, because the family plays a key role in governing Nilotic society. Established family law is a part of the larger political order. Family rules generally reflect recognized social values. In a Nilotic family, actions consistent with principles of doing right are permitted, but wrong actions, or actions inconsistent with accepted values, are forbidden. The role a woman plays in seeking truth in every thought, word, and deed is directly related to the establishment of right living in the Nilotic family and community.

Although family rules are presumed to govern life, people do make wrong decisions that lead to wrongdoing. The misfortunes that follow are regarded as coming from God, who supports the person who has the *cuong,* the right, in the matter and punishes the person who is in the wrong. Admission of guilt and repentance are key to forgiveness and reconciliation. If neither party to a conflict admits to wrongdoing, however, it is the women who must take on the continuing role of monitoring future threats to peace and of collaborating with traditional leaders and those concerned with religious and educational efforts to bring peace to a situation.

The dynamic of mutual respect between Nilotic men and women, coupled with the expectation that truth telling is necessary for right relationships, clearly holds potential as an engine for driving grassroots peacemaking forward. The potential is illustrated by two common, yet powerful Nilotic proverbs. One says: The fearless man is a danger to his kin, but he is also a security to his kin. This means that while a fearless man can cause trouble, he is also prized because he protects his family. The other says: No matter how powerful he is, a man cannot have children without a woman; for if a wife rolls up her belongings and goes back to her family, where will her husband get children?

The Akobo Peace Conference

By the end of July 1994, the continuing development of grassroots networks and organizations in Upper Nile had significantly enhanced inter-community communications and peace efforts, inevitably leading to the formation of a major peace conference. Several outside organizations, including the Presbyterian Church, offered financial and technical support for the conference. Peace was becoming a reality to the Jikany and Lou Nuer.

From mid August to late September 1994, people gathered for a conference in Akobo, the major town in the region. The official conference of 500 members included an assembly of invited delegates and eighteen delegations of mediators. The conference itself modeled an innovative, participatory approach to conflict resolution. Support for the conference was so widespread that over 5,000 people came to Akobo to participate. The conference itself lasted forty-five days.

The design of the Akobo Peace Conference reflected the Nuer way of conflict resolution, which is grounded in concepts of covenantal relationships and mutual understanding and based on principles of equality and fairness in daily affairs. To develop a greater understanding of social processes associated with community structures in Nuerland, several organizations monitored and observed the proceedings.

The organization of the conference included ad-hoc committees, and hearings based upon the traditional court. There was a technical committee that analyzed issues and made recommendations. There also was a secretariat to chair the conference.

The Nilotic belief about conflict is that conflict must be resolved by involving others, usually elders. The Nilotic people adore their elders, especially one who is a reasonable man with a reputation for choosing the sensible solution and recognizing the necessary direction to take for peaceful negotiation and rational behavior in the community. Malual Wun Kuoth, an elder drawing on forty-four years of experience as a chief, was selected to preside as secretariat of the conference.

It is important to keep in mind that leading up to the conference, people first had to admit that there was a problem that needed to be resolved. The Nuer recognize that within the community there is space to disagree and argue. They know that they have to live together and they understand the continuing possibility of reconciliation. They know that there will be time and resources devoted to resolving a matter of conflict. But without first acknowledging mistakes, the process cannot begin. To hold back may cause harm to oneself and to the community. In the Nuer community, there are no winners or losers; there is always room for compromise. Therefore, besides the structure of the conference itself, the most important factor at Akobo was the readiness of the Lou and the Jikany Nuer to resolve their differences. The two communities came together seeking forgiveness as the basis for reconciliation.

The conference was designed to gather information that supported reconciliation. The role of

Nilotic women during this kind of conflict resolution is to pressure the disparate groups to to openly discuss the issues. Women played a big role in gathering the necessary information at Akobo. The conference was structured so that anyone could ask questions or make statements from the floor. During the public discussion, women banded together in such a way that men could not lie about their wrongdoing. Often, the women had been the sole witnesses to the abuses committed by armed men. The women told stories that brought the offenders to their knees. They described specific incidences of rape; of killing women, children, and the elderly; of stealing cattle; and of the destruction of community properties.

The purpose of the conference was to restore stability, so that communities could rebuild. But the dialogue was on such a scale that, especially for the women, the proceedings broke new ground in providing information of value to future reconciliation processes.

The Jikany and the Lou Nuer women acted upon their shared belief that truth brings peace and reconciliation between communities. Women of both clans told me that if their communities were to have peace, then all concerned must tell the whole truth. Representatives of local grassroots women's groups converged on the Jikany-Lou peace conference to tell stories about their common daily struggle to meet basic needs. They spoke out with the intention of moving the conflict toward resolution. These women, many of whom were not accustomed to speaking in public, stood bravely in front of large audiences, telling their stories and challenging the men who had been involved in the fighting. Women of opposing clans stood together, supporting each other whenever one came forward to speak. "*Laa re, laa re, nyamar*," they called out. "Tell it, tell it, my sister!"

Mary Nyakang Chol (Nyachol) is one example. She was the leader of the Ayot women's group. When Nyachol took her turn at the microphone, she pointed her finger in the direction of Chairman Malual Wun Kuoth. She said to the crowd, "*Gor nei rami ci duer laat, ka jen cuong bi mal nongo. Neme e laatdan kon maan.* We want to identify those who did wrong. It is only truth that can bring peace. This is the women's job." I was overwhelmed by Nyachol's courage in rising to the challenge to become a strong figure in the community.

Nyachol and the other women at the Akobo conference were fact-finders, providing information useful to moving forward the process of resolving the larger conflict. Their words reminded me of the things I used to hear from my mother when she urged my sisters and me never to lie. My mother told us to always tell the truth, regardless of the obstacles. "So, girl," Mother would say, "don't you lie now. Don't you open your mouth with something that is going to cause you a problem all your life. Be a strong woman and let it all out, because someday you are going to be a mother. And mothers can tell only the truth."

Men who did not want to be exposed as liars by the women were forced to the truth in public. "You better tell what happened, or else I am going to tell it all," was the clear, strong message from the women to the men. "Tell the whole truth."

At the end of forty-five days of truth telling, the communities came to forgiveness and agreement on the terms of restitution. As a result of open discussions among the delegates, there was agreement over the use of common-pool resources such as water, fishing areas, and grazing grounds. At the conclusion of the peace conference in Akobo, the ritual was performed of shedding the blood of the white bull and sharing a meal to seal the peace agreement.

The resolution of the Jikany-Lou conflict shows that among the Nuer, as among other Nilotic communities in the region, strength lies in the amicable cooperation of the members of different lineages and clans. As the Nilotic people say, "We can fight, and we can negotiate, when need be."

After Akobo: Women Voices for Peace

It is one thing to agree to make peace and yet another thing to keep the peace. The peacekeeping process was given a boost in eastern Upper Nile Region when the liberation movement faction called the South Sudan Independence Movement/Army (SSIM/A) passed a resolution at its Akobo Convention of 1994 giving women's organizations free access to the region and assuring their safe passage to promote grassroots peace in the SSIM/A controlled areas. SSIM/A leader Dr. Riek Machar and his commanders kept the peace and stability in the region according to the Akobo reconciliation, while the United Nations' agencies and non-governmental organizations (NGOs) provided leadership training to communities, women's organizations, and local churches to enable them to better govern themselves and run the affairs of their villages. Alongside this effort, local churches and women's groups worked to develop community-based organizations that could provide effective channels through which local communities could receive messages and peace education.

The success of the Akobo Peace Conference encouraged other groups in southern Sudan to seek grassroots solutions to their problems. Across southern Sudan, women began organizing to find alternative solutions to inter-factional conflict. Peace, reconciliation, and forgiveness among their communities were their primary objectives. The women tried to stop the violence that was destroying their way of life and devoted their energies to keeping families intact. For Nilotic women, making peace means figuring out how to meet economic, social, and spiritual needs. The women usually put aside their differences and come together as one, because they need each other to survive.

I believe that the breakthrough in halting the inter-faction fighting across southern Sudan came about because of the unity we now see among the women. The beginnings of this unity can be traced back to the success of the Akobo Peace Conference. Shortly after the conference, for example, in late 1994, the village of Akot in the Lakes Region where I grew up experienced an especially brutal inter-factional battle. Ayada my niece was one of the innocent victims of the violence. Before their physical wounds had healed, the women of Akot began taking the step of adopting the Akobo strategy to raise peace awareness within their communities. My older sister Martha Apanda organized women in her church. They called themselves "Mothers for Peace." This group since has become one of the leading women's organizations advocating peace.

Nevertheless, the success of the grassroots peace movement is still overshadowed by the larger conflict. Nearly two decades of civil war have had a traumatic and devastating impact on families.

Government of Sudan (GOS) and SPLA/M attacks on civilians still are a major problem all over the South. The SPLA/M commanders, who fear united local resistance to their Marxist policies, have deliberately played families and clans against one another. Now, in one family out of three, the breadwinner is a woman. More and more women are becoming the sole food producers, working from dawn to dusk to cultivate crops and gather wild plants to feed their children. Many trek for two or more hours a day in search of water and firewood. This is why restoring stability among the Lou and Jikany communities was crucial to the survival of women in that region, especially the widows, who depend upon either a brother or a male cousin for support.

In the Upper Nile area, cooperatives have been formed in which women work as partners in vegetable gardens along the rivers. For the South Sudan Women's Association (SSWA) and the Presbyterian Women of Sudan (PWOS) in Upper Nile, finding solutions to the lack of food, medicine, and security remains the overwhelming concern. Extending the women's traditional food gathering strategy to include farming has been one of the most reliable methods of increasing domestic food supplies. This change reduced the long hours women were spending hunting wild plants and fruit. As women saw the obvious benefit of growing their own foods, they also reduced the time spent brewing and selling beer in favor of doing more fieldwork to raise food production.

In early 1997, I went back to southern Sudan to evaluate the progress of the grassroots peace movement. The reports I heard from women in the Upper Nile areas and in Kenyan refugee camps showed that the peace education had been successful in achieving its objectives. The peace education program had benefited from the participation of resource persons, men and women originally from the Upper Nile area, who had returned from the United Kingdom, the United States of America, and Egypt to work with their people.

Several communities in southern Sudan, notably the Lou and the Jikany Nuer, had made major leaps toward improving their shared use of common resources, such as water, grazing land, forest, and fishing grounds.

On this visit, I observed three major spin-offs of the Akobo Peace Conference. The first was the proliferation of people talking about peacemaking. The second was the re-establishment of traditional and modern civic structures and the third was the formation by the SSIM/A of mobile peace committees that included clergy and male and female community leaders. Members of the mobile peace committees spent most of their time at the fishing and cattle camps, monitoring the peace. They formed a network with the local custodians (chiefs) in assessing the condition of the peace process within different communities.

The women's groups held peace education meetings. During these meetings, participants were encouraged to engage in a series of discussions on using traditional methods of conflict resolution. The southern Sudanese women who had already engaged in this work served as role models. They were able to share how many communities in the Upper Nile area were continuing their peace work, while others were changing their attitudes toward hostile groups. Not only the women, but also across the board, people were becoming aware of the power they held in approaching conflict resolution using the traditional means of open group discussion.

Many people have asked me to describe my role in organizing the women for peace. I think my role was not something that I created, but rather it was something that I discovered. During my childhood, I believed that my African culture was in conflict with my modern ways. But gradually, I began to understand that to move forward in life, I must synthesize all of my learning and skills. In organizing the women, I knew that I had to become one of them. But sometimes I needed a reminder.

One day during my 1997 visit, I was walking three miles to reach the village of Nyandiit to attend a women's peace meeting with Nyaber my sister in-law. Nyaber was an elected member of the South Sudanese Women's Association (SSWA). She had attended the 1994 Akobo Peace Conference and had testified to what she had witnessed when armed Lou Nuer attacked and burned the town of Nasir.

As we walked along, Nyaber was telling me about her experience at the Akobo Conference. I was not listening. I was impatient to reach the women's peace meeting. "Nyaber, *ber wan nee!* Come on, let's go!" I yelled.

But Nyaber would not be hurried. "At first," she said, "I didn't understand the role I was supposed to play in the gathering at Akobo. So I thought, well, I am going to go in there and sit down and wait. The men are going to tell us what to do."

Suddenly I heard what Nyaber was saying. Suddenly I wondered why I was trotting along in such an all-out American hurry. I had not come to Africa to tell these women what to do.

In the Nilotic culture, the role of women requires an understanding of group dynamics and skill in building a consensus. The women have to sort through the confusion, the ambiguities, and the contradictions of conflict. The appropriate structures for conflict resolution are the local social networks and the web of relatives, friends, and acquaintances that surrounds each person. These social networks are useful vehicles for organized women's activities because the mutual understandings, shared values, and common perspectives that they foster enable women to work together. This is why my role is to become one of them. We are women working together.

Today Nyaber is part of a large group of women in southern Sudan that has been working for peace. Even today as I write this story, Nyaber and other Sudanese women are combining old and new ways to make peace at the grassroots level. They are walking from village to village and cattle camp to cattle camp, spreading the message of peace to the members of their communities.

Interaction with role models is particularly useful in helping the women envision the possibilities of combining family responsibilities with community leadership. This is why I place an emphasis on developing women's leadership potential; on building self-esteem, assertiveness, and self-confidence; and on elevating the status of women's organizations. As women maintain their traditional value of telling the truth, they become a force for driving the peace forward.

Nyabiel was an elected leader from Yaui village. She became a very strong woman leader in the region. Whenever she told her story, it had much influence on women, especially the widows. She would open with *mäle*, or peace, the traditional greeting:

> "*Mäle.* Peace. *E han ret.* I am a widow. I lost my husband in inter-factional fighting in 1992. I am a member of the South Sudan Women Association (SSWA). I have not had any schooling, but I learned about committee work through a women's' organization. I have attended many women's peace meetings and we have learned a lot from our sister Julia who has come back to be with us at this difficult time. In the women's organizations, representatives are elected, so I was elected to represent my village. It is not difficult to learn from a person who speaks the same language as you do. This has been very encouraging to us, and it is our duty as mothers to bring peace to our communities."

Peace education has now been instituted as a continuing activity on the South Sudan Women's Association calendar, and an ad-hoc committee was formed to continue with peace education activities and networking. The committee represents all of the women's groups, religious and non-religious.

One activity the SSWA pushed for was the revival of traditional rituals of conflict resolution in southern Sudanese communities. For example, the Acholi people of eastern Equatoria have a reconciliation ritual very similar to that of the Nuer. When there has been a conflict and people realize that the parties in conflict must be reconciled, they all must drink the juice of the *oput* plant. The *oput* plant never grows by itself; it grows only in groups. It is a communal plant. Drinking the juice of this plant squeezed into water signifies that the reconciling parties understand that they cannot live by themselves. They then make a solemn promise never to fight again. This is similar to the Nuer rituals of using the blood of an animal or eating meat from the same animal as a solemn promise never to cause harm again, because blood represent life to the Nilotic people. This ritual of blood and sharing of meat was performed in Akobo in order to seal the agreement.

In one peace meeting I attended not long after Akobo, the women reported on their work and the progress they had made. They stressed the importance of maintaining traditional ways of life. Rituals are a key to maintaining peace, because the violation of one's pledge of peace is believed to be a form of self-destruction. A woman told the group, "It is ten months and peace is holding. This is good, because people believe in the wisdom of the elders and those who went before them. What has helped us is that the Nuer people stick to their rituals because the elders perform them. You have to know that something is forbidden, you have to be wise not to violate the prohibition, because you never know what might happen to you if you disobey."

As my 1997 visit drew to a close, before returning to the United States I went to visit the Dinka women who were in Lokichokio, Kenya, at the International Red Cross Hospital. Because my mother is Dinka and my father Nuer, I have links to both groups of women in southern Sudan. I am not a stranger to the land of my mother, the place of my birth. The Dinka women once celebrated my birth. The are the ones who introduced me to a woman's life and my role and duties.

From the sick and wounded Dinka women in the hospital, I learned that the peace and forgiveness among Nuer groups of Upper Nile was presenting an encouraging and positive model for other communities in southern Sudan. I told the women in the hospital about what I had seen in the Nuer areas and they were happy and asked me to visit their villages too. One Dinka woman said,

> "We all want peace. We need to provide for our families. As mothers, we have to join together and work through this larger, Dinka-Nuer conflict. Because we don't have networks, women are not able to meet with their sisters in the Western Nuerland to work together. We must stop this whole Nuer-Dinka conflict. It is important that we begin working now. We must show our commitment to peace. The Nuer and the Dinka must have peace. My sisters, we have seen what modern weapons have done to us. And the old people, who were so much a part of us, have all gone."

"No," I thought as I looked at the women around me. "As long as there are women like this who want peace for their families, the old people always will be very much a part of us."

Why Indigenous Peace-building Matters

Women long have been considered stumbling blocks to progress, or else as conservative elements holding back social change. This is because the life of the woman, revolving as it does around child raising and the hearth, seems to remain relatively unchanged from generation to generation. But with the war in southern Sudan, women's lives have changed dramatically. A woman's survival is now in her own hands, and the only means left to her is to make peace. If southern Sudanese women yearn for the past and cherish their traditions, it is because the traditions and the past belong to them. The woman in Nilotic society, and especially among the Nuer, is the producer of life itself, the mother of children. Indeed, life goes on and on for the Nilotic woman, no matter how it falls apart for the man.

My dream is to bring back the peace-seeking heritage of the Nilotic people. I want the change to start from the bottom up, to move from the household outward. When I started working with the women, I had a feeling that they would be the first to be affected by the transforming power of new ideas.

My ultimate purpose in working with the women is to improve the overall situation of communities in southern Sudan. I want to focus attention on fundamental needs such as literacy, clean water, vocational literacy, and health care. In southern Sudan, people want to do things themselves. They want to be self-reliant and they want to control their own lives.

Institution building, including human resource development, is at the center of the strategy I use to train women's group leaders. As the women gain an understanding of the ideological differences among the southern Sudanese factions, they are able to address peace processes in a more meaningful way.

But training and institution building are not the only needs. The people of southern Sudan cannot acquire the skills that will help them rebuild their lives when they first must struggle everyday simply to find clean drinking water and to produce something to eat.

The efforts of the grassroots women in rural southern Sudan are representative of a larger segment of the population wanting peace. What we have learned can be applied to the broader conflict resolution process.

The grassroots women of southern Sudan, sustained by their own inner strength, felt that the risks were worth taking and that the hardships were merely something to get through on the way to achieving peace. I believe that only those who are willing to take these risks can bring peace and freedom to others. Endurance in the face of obstacles is needed during this period of transition and insecurity. And endurance is one thing that the women have.

Despite significant barriers to achievement, the women persist in seeking peace. With little outside support, they keep going. They do what their mothers taught them to do: seek the truth and tell the truth.

Meeting with a group of women in Akobo.

Chapter IX

My Own Search for Truth

We will not be satisfied until justice
rolls down like waters and
righteousness like a mighty stream.
Martin Luther King, Jr.

Why I Must Speak Out

My mother had a saying that suited every situation in our lives. She said, "*Ran jam yiith en-ee ran bi piir.* Telling the truth is the best way to make life." This was the rule of our home and my mother was our teacher. Now it is my duty to pass on this tradition to my daughters and to other Nilotic women. My mother always said, "Mothers do not lie. They tell the truth, and truth is what gives courage."

The stories of people's lives in the war zone of southern Sudan are full of tears and heartache and courage. The tales of the starving, the sick, the displaced, and the untold suffering of my people remind me of the Nilotic traditional belief that envisions a turbulent world constantly seeking a timeless peace. The Nilotic people say, "human life is not a smooth stream flowing through time, but it is like the River Nile in the raining seasons: restless, interminably rising and falling, even while seeking its own level."

The river tells the truth.

My own life is like the river. It rises and falls on the unstoppable courage of my people and on my own search for truth in the face of tragedy.

From books I learned about Nelson Mandela, Mother Teresa, and others who devoted their lives to the cause of justice and freedom for mankind. After reading about Gandhi's approach to civil disobedience, I began to like the idea of nonviolent action, both as a philosophy and as a technique of political strategy. The Russian Count Leo Tolstoy's *The Kingdom of God Is Within You* helped me shape my feelings into clear thoughts. This work presented the idea of "nonresistance to evil by force" as a basic teaching of Christianity. I had personally experienced Tolstoy's observation that "the progressive movement of humanity does not proceed from the better elements in society seizing power and making those who are subject to them better, by forcible means, as both conservatives and revolutionists imagine." I knew from experience that "when whole nations have been subjugated by a new religion, and have become Christian or Mohammedan, such a conversion has never been brought about because the authorities made it obligatory...nations, on the contrary, who have been driven by force to accept the faith of their conquerors have always remained antagonistic to it."

But the idea of nonviolent ation also raised questions. Because Tolstoy's writings strengthened pacifist sentiments in Britain during the 1930s, I thought very hard about why, in the face of the clear Nazi threat, students at Oxford and Cambridge Universities had pledged "never again to fight for king and country." What, I wondered, did their protest achieve other than to encourage Hitler? I did not believe that people should submit to cruel leaders, like

Hitler, Idi Amin of Uganda, or Pol Pot of Cambodia. Amin killed most of the educated people in his country. I believed that communities must be prepared to defend themselves against such mass murderers. I believed that we must beware of the tyrant.

In the case of southern Sudan today, the majority of the Dinka people don't really know what John Garang, the notorious leader of SPLA, really thinks. They don't really know how he treats groups who are non-Dinka or people who disagree with him. This ignorance among the Dinka is one of the great barriers to resolving both the conflict among the southern liberation movement factions and the larger North/South conflict in the Sudan.

As a mother, the suffering I have seen among my people especially upsets me. I am always asking myself, "what can we do to stop this war?" Force and violence do not seem to solve anything in the long run. And neither does allowing tyranny to prosper.

As an African, my search for answers led me to study the nationalist movements that ended colonial rule. The first African patriot to receive world recognition was Dr. Kwame Nkrumah of Ghana. Dr. Nkrumah was an advocate of nonviolent civil disobedience and self-rule, as were many other Africans who led nationalist movements during the 1950s and 1960s. Their success in bringing about peaceful change helped make nonviolence a growing moral force during the twentieth century. Nevertheless, the shortcomings of these leaders while in power indicate that we still have much to learn.

On some level, I will always struggle to reconcile the ideals of my faith with the demands of reality. But I believe that the words of the Rev. Dr. Martin Luther King Jr. speak the truth, and that gives me courage. In the United States during the 1950s and 1960s, Dr. King led the nonviolent civil rights movement protest against racial segregation. This was a difficult struggle, but I believe it succeeded in bringing about change because Dr. King's actions were consistent with his Christian beliefs. He did not preach violence, but rather said that "in the process of gaining our rightful place we must not be guilty of wrongful deeds...we must never allow our creative protest to degenerate into physical violence...we must rise to the majestic heights of meeting physical force with soul force."

The Challenges Ahead

I am committed to joining hands with Africans of my generation to build a community in which peace and prosperity are goals set for life. This does not mean that we Africans should escape our African-ness and replace it with European-ness. African culture and identity is both with us and in us. We have been fed on it, brought up on it, and we will die in it. It is who we are. It is the source of our values and of the languages in which we express ourselves. And for African women, our African-ness sustains our identification as the Mothers of Mankind.

Africans must seek the truth and tell the truth. We are told that the cause of the breakdown in African social morality is easy to identify. We are told that the cause is colonialism. We are told that the cause is the cultural conflict resulting from Western values impinging on African traditional values. We are told that the root cause is the capitalist economic system of industrialized nations, which is exploiting African nations.

We must stop blaming others for our problems. We must stop demanding that others change so that we then can be happy. We must take responsibility for the development of our own African societies. We must put things right.

We cannot escape conflict. There is no place on earth that is without conflict. Conflict is not the problem.

I left Africa and came to the United States with the hope of finding peace, but in the United States I found conflict. I found a society with wide access to weapons and opportunities to use them. But I found a people who look to the processes of law, rather than to violence, as the way to resolve conflict and bring about change. This attitude of self-governance makes all the difference. In my own understanding, conflict is a part of life. But it does not have to lead to violence. We can learn how to resolve conflict by considering and involving others in the resolution process. Collectively, communities can learn to modify the underlying assumptions and rules of life which govern the way they interact with one another.

An essential element in ending violence is increasing our own and others' awareness of the deeply embedded, structural foundations of violence. Each of us must become aware of the degree to which we have embraced dehumanizing attitudes in our own behavior and in our institutions. To make progress towards peace, we must focus on our own values, attitudes, and behaviors. We have placed too much emphasis on reforming others. Violence is in our minds when we do not base our conduct on principles firmly rooted in ethical traditions and in respect for one another as human beings.

People all over the world have contributed to violence by accepting principles that have dehumanized others. Sometimes, it is difficult to see how this happens. We would rather not answer the question, "and who is my neighbor?" But if we are to preserve life, we must answer that question and we must answer it truthfully.

It is not easy to accept the reality of the destruction that we Sudanese have done to one another; we have killed each other and allowed hunger and disease to kill our people. We must change our ways.

There is much that needs to be done. The basic antidotes to violence are genuine respect for other people as equals and peaceful means of reconciliation of differences. These moral truths can be learned from experience, but for many they gain added power as tenets of faith. The Nilotic principle of equality for all people is known as *Gaat Kouth*, or God's children. We are God's creation. Those Africans who still believe in their ancestors and in the spirit of creation will have to begin by asking for forgiveness. They should begin with these words of prayer, "God of my ancestors, forgive us for doing evil against our fellow humans. We are all one in your creation; guide us to respect and help one another so we can live in peace."

Making peace is overcoming violence. Violence results from the desire of individuals and communities to dominate others, and from a refusal to share resources and political power. The struggle to dominate and control has polarized peoples around the world in every dimension imaginable. Conflict emerges between rich and poor, industrialized countries and developing ones, men and women, landlords and tenants, skilled laborers and unskilled, indigenous communities and migrant, believers and non-believers, conservative and liberal, racial groups, religious groups, and on and on. Any one of these differences, when allowed to become an un-reconciled polarization, can lead to violence.

In the long term, overcoming violence and resolving conflict must be based on changing individual attitudes and assuring equality, justice, and freedom for all humanity. This is the only way we can live in peace with all kinds of people, regardless of their political, religious, ethnic, racial, and national identities.

The values held by individuals and communities are gradually woven into the formal and informal institutions by which they live and relate to each other. In most cultures, the values which people hold are derived from religious heritage or experience. "Democratic societies," Professor Vincent Ostrom of Indiana University says, "are based on wide acceptance of moral values and the development of morally grounded institutions."

Generally, the values expressed in law, education, religion, family, work, the media, and the economy of a society are the values that the majority professes to believe. Those of us who claim allegiance to the values of equality, justice, and freedom frequently deny the dignity of others by our personal behavior. We would be peacemakers, but too often we rely on force as our first resort and always as the ultimate resort for confronting conflict.

I want to instill a sense of a "community of peace" in my people, but not by force. I know that I must lead by example. I must show the women that they must not sit and wait for peace to happen; they must go out and do something for themselves.

Coming to the United States changed my whole life. It offered me the opportunity to achieve a higher level of education, which gave me a broader vision of life. It also gave me the opportunity to learn the most important aspect of life, the art of relating to other people. This insight gave me a desire to stand apart, to examine even the way I see myself, and to listen and learn from others. It has helped me to better deal with my own daily problems and with women in southern Sudan who were struggling to survive.

I became involved in the process of organizing women for peacemaking in 1994, when the Jikany/Lou Nuer conflict was out of control. At that time, life had become such a struggle that it was not easy for either the women or me to define our roles. But we operated within guidelines that had been established for generations in the minds of Sudanese people. Before I established discussion groups among the women, I asked them about gender relations and how we might approach them without causing conflict. The women said they wanted to recover the faith of their husbands and improve and build stronger relationships with them. From this starting point, the women were able to emphasize the importance of peace among the different ethnic communities. Their efforts deserve praise. The success of women's activities in both establishing a better rapport with their husbands, and in furthering women's grassroots work, was evidenced in the women's discussion groups, since the majority of women received support from their husbands to participate in the women's groups. The men took care of the children while the women attended meetings.

After the peace conference, as my own role in the peace education training evolved, I worked with the women who were to lead women's peace committees in their villages. These women were to organize the women's meetings, and I would be there to advise and counsel on different issues. I advocated dialogue to start the process because this would help us to listen and seek understanding of one another's viewpoints. This dialogue would lay a foundation upon which to build understanding and trust among the individuals and groups, and to reduce escalation of conflict.

I had established a relationship with almost every member of the grassroots women's peace effort in the Upper Nile region. Networking opened the lines of communication. Face-to-face talks made it easy for women to cooperate with each other. This process was very effective because it was backed up by my sharing my writing with the women and giving them the opportunity to take the lead. Some women told me that they had read some of my reports. They said they had also read them aloud, translating into the Nuer and Dinka languages, to those who could not read and write.

The group discussions indicate how the procedural arrangements that evolved within our grassroots organizations were used to build better personal relationships among the women. The goal was to provide both opportunities for informal interaction among women and for participation in peacemaking. Members of the discussion groups offered suggestions to one another for following up their work. One woman told me that she found the group discussions helpful and felt the discussions allowed the women to work as a team.

I tried to help women see alternative ways of looking at situations. They had to explore issues in their own areas, determined by their own needs and interests. Each step was taken only after a fair amount of discussion among the women's group as to how we should proceed and what the likely effects of the activities would be. By the end of the peace education training, each woman had participated in six different sessions, with each session building on the information they had previously received.

The women were not only comfortable with what I did, but they have been generally complimentary about my approach. Today, I describe my approach as people-centered. I find ways to facilitate the women in identifying and discussing issues that concern them. This approach is one that the women appreciated and praised. Women have said over and over, "you looked upon us as your sisters, friends, and equals." I treated the women, to some extent, as resource persons from whom I could learn about the ways of people and became a better messenger about their ways of life.

This was a genuine, collaborative peace making process. I simply told the women what I knew or what I thought, and they reciprocated. I was pleasantly surprised by how well things turned out. My work might have gone differently, of course, but I like to think that by sticking to my principles and by allowing the women to lead their own work and to make their own decisions, we made progress.

The next challenge will be finding a few brave individuals in northern and southern Sudan who are willing to join a common quest for harmony and understanding. The stability and peace of any society depends on a sense of security within each component community. Members must be free to observe the cultural and ritual obligations of their spiritual beliefs with no constraint on the part of political authorities.

Both the *Qu'ran* and the *Bible* have the aspects of a tradition which support an appeal to reason and respect for others. They abound with messages exhorting peace, love, justice and mercy.

We Sudanese we ought to be asking ourselves how we are going to make the Sudan into a country where all can be equal citizens. Indeed, *can* we create a Sudanese society where Sudanese of different colors, different beliefs, and different cultures all unite by our common humanity?

It is my belief and my conviction that the first step is an honest acknowledging of the naked problems afflicting us as Sudanese and as human beings. We have to accept that, whether unwittingly or through sheer negligence, carelessness, or greed, we have allowed the situation in Sudan to go too far. We Sudanese people have not taken the time to tackle our problems with integrity and seriousness. We have not accepted our responsibility as citizens, but rather have behaved as subjects.

We Southerners have to look to our past to find peace; we have to learn from the time when socio-cultural harmony was the order of the day. We must begin to educate young Sudanese to have self-confidence, and revive the Sudanese who have been convinced through Western or Islamic education that their cultural system and values are inferior. I am ashamed of those educated Sudanese, who are foreigners in their own land, who unthinkingly and shamelessly copy other cultural values instead of creating to their own. My cry here is that we must identify our weaknesses in not finding solutions to the civil war. We must institute measures to overcome these weaknesses. Nilotic people have the potential to make conflict constructive and manageable by making the effort to understand each other.

The greatest challenge for the Sudanese people is choosing the right path for Sudan as a nation. During the last century, brave men and women struggled to get rid of colonialism. It was the privilege of my generation to be the new citizens of an independent nation. With independence, we enjoyed the birth of a republic. It meant the birth of an anthem and the implantation of a flag—with green for the land, gold for the peace, and blue for the Nile—representing treasures given to the Sudanese by nature. (President Nimeiry later changed the flag to red, white, black, and green).

We have heard again and again from Sudanese leaders that all forces in the country should be combined and mobilized to build the nation. These words did not translate into reality; instead, our nation turned into a bleeding, suffering land. It seemed that all we had learned was how to kill people and throw their bodies into the Nile River. We did not use its water to meet the requirements of life; instead we used it as a burial ground to feed the crocodiles.

The Sudanese people are struggling over the concepts of justice and equality. There is widespread disagreement about some of the arrangements that are considered just in the Sudan. The majority of Sudanese, especially those in the North, strongly agree that Islam and its law *Shari'a* are the way to guide decisions in the everyday lives of all Sudanese.

In Sudan the notion of "justice" in the society has clearly been dominated by the Islamic-Arab North, whose religious leaders, like the Pharisees of Jesus' day, have led the people into a morass of symbolism and rituals bearing little resemblance to teaching of the

Holy *Qur'an*. These leaders' discussions of justice conjure up debates over minuscule points of orthodoxy.

Islam in Sudan has been used as an instrument to oppress the population. It has been used to create legislation that rejects other points of view. The writing of Mahmud Muhammad Taha of the Republican Brothers has inspired many young northern Sudanese to challenge the northern sectarian leaders who claim Islam's destiny is dominance. Taha's conception of Islam emphasized "the moral principles of the Meccan texts of the *Qur'an* at the expense of the legal codes implemented in Medina, which are seen as less universal and more related to time and place." He advocated a re-definition of the historical *Shari'a* with an emphasis on religious freedom and social equality. Taha's vision for Islam appeared to hold the potential for peace in the Sudan. In the 1970s, thousands of Sudanese Muslims and Christians supported his approach and admired Taha for his integrity and consistency about human relations.

Taha's teaching raised many fundamental questions in Sudanese politics. He sought to reconcile Islam with human equality, justice, religious freedom, and political democracy. He rejected cultural and religious notions of Arab-Islamic hegemony and argued for the necessity of a democratic system to ensure the equality of all Sudanese, regardless of their religious beliefs, gender and race. He used the *Qur'anic* verse: *lasta 'alaihim bi-musaitir* (you are not to dictate them) arguing that the Prophet Muhammad had no mandate to impose Islam on anyone.

Taha's approach to the Sudanese problem is an important lesson to those who are seeking peace. He encouraged all believers, including Christians and

Muslims, to seek dialogue with one another. The Republican Brothers and southern Sudanese often found common ground for cooperation on many issues. Both groups have always supported peace and they have worked for the reconciliation of Christians and Muslims in the Sudan. Sudanese people not only learned form Taha's message, but he gave them tools that are capable of shedding light upon Sudanese human relations. He taught the Sudanese people to stand against injustices, and to work together to make peace. Taha stood against injustice, and was executed because of his beliefs.

Ending violence requires spiritual understanding. It has become a frustration to me when the natural instinct for spiritual orientation is turned aside by cold drafts of agnosticism and atheism. If life really is a senseless existence on an aging planet in a meaningless and possibly dying universe, then human fate is not tragic. It is not even absurd. It is simply, and in the most devastating psychological terms, inconsequential. That the pounding egos of humanity find it difficult to accept such a possibility is not strange.

What is strange is that in a scientific age, people are still so uncertain about human relations and the basic meaning of life. For, with all of the mythic character of any traditional theology, whether Islamic or Judeo-Christian, it is surely conceivable that the religiously sensitive mind may be tapping a source and dimension of reality. There are a sufficient number of friendly signs in human basic principles of existence— love, compassion, a sense of injustice, commitment to principle, beauty, art, music, poetry, the delights of intellectual discovery—to make the notion of complete absurdity itself completely absurd.

Indeed, despite their difference in religious belief and ritual, Jews, Christians, Muslims, and Nilotic peoples all believe in a Creator God. But the way things have been happening in Sudan, the majority of Sudanese would claim that there is no single approach to social justice that is generally applicable.

For centuries, the Judeo-Christian-Islamic tradition brought to millions of people in Africa a spiritual orientation and moral purpose. Many Africans still hold to the conceptual icons of their traditions, and an even larger number find intermittent solace and inspiration in the words and lives of prophets and saints. That the Judeo-Christian tradition continues to accommodate the African beliefs in creation and the spirit is a tribute to the power of their religious insights, imageries, and poetry to nourish and inform mankind's instinct for spiritual orientation.

Furthermore, the inner peace that comes from disciplined mediation, the increasing evidence of thought transference, the heightened probability of conscious existence in other galaxies and planetary systems all raise at least the possibility that the universe is far friendlier than the either/or orientation presently conveyed by those who believe they have been given a mandate to direct human lives. The search for a sense of belonging in one's universal home is not an inconsequential religious task. It is, on the contrary, an ultimate condition for reestablishing, for vast numbers of people, a sense of hope and purpose in life.

If we recognize that we are capable of all virtues and all vices occurring in other people, we will be able to view problems with sincerity, rather than always trying to find a scapegoat for our ills.

Time is running out. We must reconcile the various differences confronting us. The defense of orthodoxy must not be had at the expense of humanity. We have done enough violence. It is time to make peace.

Becoming a Messenger about the Ways of People's Lives

My life's story is one of struggle and hope. I have seen my people, who once were handsome, become ugly, emaciated skeletons. I have been close when people have been murdered and women raped. I have seen women lose their children. I know young people who have gone astray and are killing their own people. I have seen this horror over and over in my nightmares and it seems to have no end. The killing I have seen in southern Sudan has made life a nightmare for me. I say to my children, "I have seen a lot of my people—the babies, the young, and the old—all gone, and still more are dying." But life goes on, and that is one reason why my mother always said that it is good to be alive.

My position as a Nilotic woman is at the center of the family. This position is a focal point and is emotionally rich. It is rooted in the values of the Nilotic culture, which are values of the heart. They include a sense of connection to others, a concern for the common good, the courage to seek justice, and a devotion to one's community. In this world I have achieved a certain peace within myself, but I think the seeking after the inner sense of truth will never cease in me. My life proves that I belong to and have a place in the Nilotic society. I cannot escape the "togetherness" of the Nilotic life. The concerns about my people are paramount in my mind.

My challenge, and the challenge for all southern Sudanese, is to think beyond short-term solutions to the Sudan problem. We must work toward long-term solutions. We cannot give up the effort of making peace simply because we think the problems are too deeply embedded in our society. Change is always possible.

I will continue to speak for my people and seek social transformation at this time of crisis. This is a big task and often frustrating, because change is a gradual process. I will continue because to keep on working for social justice, building peace, and struggling to transform inequalities is more than a means to an end. It is an end in and of itself, because peace is a total way of life.

I will continue to ask, "Who am I? What does my life mean to my people, my country, and my world?"

I will continue to forge an understanding of myself and the world around me.

I am an African.

A Sudanese.

A Nilotic from southern Sudan.

A Nuer from Lou.

A Gon from Rumjok section.

A woman.

A mother.

Even though I have lived in the United States for a long time, I cannot lose sight of the community of which I am a part. I still think like an African; I still worship like an African. I still embrace African traditions, sing African songs, dance African dances, and cook African dishes. The values that I acquired in my childhood always bring me back to the ways of my people.

At times I may struggle to understand myself and the world around me. But I always understand that my role as a woman and a mother is to provide nurture, care, and support for my people.

There is no call more worthy than this one.

Bibliography

_____. Amnesty International, 1993. *Sudan: A Human Tragedy in the Making.* Amnesty International.

Duany, Julia Aker. 1997. Making Peace: A Report on Grassroots Peace Efforts by Women in South Sudan. *African Journal of Institutions and Development* (AJID), Obafemi Awolowo University, Ile-Ife, Nigeria, Vol. 3 Nos. 1 & 2. pp.19-34.

Duany, Wal. 1992. "Neither Palaces Nor Prisons: The Constitution of Order Among the Nuer." Ph. D. Dissertation, Department of Political Science and School of Public and Environment Affairs, Indiana University, Bloomington.

Gluckman, Max. 1969. *Ideas and Procedures in African Customary Law.* Oxford University Press.

Lederach, J. Paul. 1995. *Preparing for Peace: Conflict Transformation Across Cultures.* Syracuse, New York. Syracuse University Press.

Mbiti, John S. 1970. *Concepts of God in Africa.* S.P.C. K.

_____ . 1969. *African Religions and Philosophy.* London Heinemann

Ostrom, Vincent. 1997. *The Meaning of Democracy and the Vulnerability of Democracies*. Ann Arbor, The University of Michigan Press.

Parsons, T. 1951. *The Social System.* London, Routledge.

Radcliffe-Brown, A. R., and Daryl Forde, eds. 1950. *African Systems of Kinship and Marriage*. New York. Oxford University Press.

Ray, Benjamin C. 1976. *African Religions*. Englewood Cliffs, N. J.

Young, T. C. 1937. *African Ways and Wisdom: A Contribution to Understanding*. London, The United Society for Christian Literature.

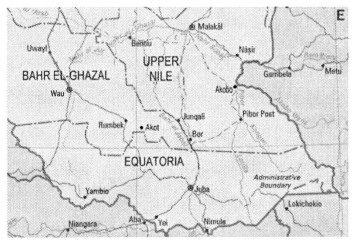

Area of Detail

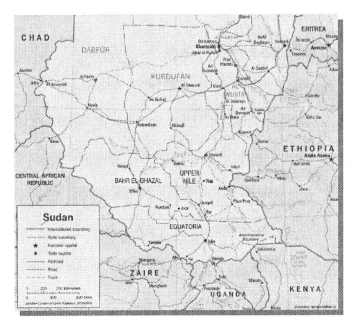

Area of Detail

255

About the Author

I hold the position of research associate at the Workshop in Political Theory and Policy Analysis at Indiana University. I earned my Ph. D. in Higher Education at Indiana University. I taught at both elementary and secondary schools in the Sudan and in the United States. My areas of interest are social and justice issues, and my recent work is in gender and conflict resolution in developing countries, particularly in Africa. I was born in a small town in South Sudan. I am a mother of five children, three boys and two girls.

Printed in the United States
68022LVS00001B/9